P9-CCF-850

Sam Hinn

Changed IN His Presence

CREATION HOUSE

BOOKS ABOUT SPIRIT-LED LIVING

ORLANDO, FLORIDA

Creation House
Strang Communications Company
600 Rinehart Road
Lake Mary, FL 32746
Fax: (407) 333-7100

First printing: September 1995
Second printing: December 1995

To my beautiful wife, Erika. When the Lord gave you to me He gave me the most beautiful gift on this earth. Thank you for giving me the greatest years of my life. If the first ten years were this great, I can't wait for the next ten. You are a gift from God, and I love you with all my heart and my life.

To my children, you are a gift of God to your mom and me. Thank you for understanding why daddy has to be gone so much.

- Samia the little worshipper, you are my honey. Samia don't ever stop worshipping the Lord. You are the song in my heart. One day baby you and I will stand to worship God together here and in eternity.

- Costi, you are my hockey buddy. Son, the Lord has his hand on you in such a special way. I can't wait for the day to come when you and I will stand and preach God's Word together, and after that we're on the ice together. I love you, and I am so proud of you.

- Michael, now you are three. Soon you will be able to read. Son, when the Lord gave you to us, He gave us the gift of joy. I love you too my little hockey, cowboy buddy. (Yippee Ki Yo Kiyay)

- Christa "anointed," before you were born, I prayed for one more girl. God gave me my heart's desire in you. He gave me a beautiful and anointed, daddy's little girl.

My heart is filled with gratitude to the One who saved and called me to Himself. All the blessings in my life have come from Him. I love Him more than life, my Savior and Lord Jesus Christ.

Acknowledgment

I want to express my deepest love to my family. God has so blessed me with having such a great family. My saintly mother who has prayed for all of us in the quiet hours of the morning while we were still sleeping, Yama God is answering your prayers (ana ba hib bic).

To my brothers Benny, Chris, William, Henry, Mike and my sisters Mary and Rose; in my heart and life I will always carry something from each of you. Thank you for giving of yourselves. I love you so much.

Phil Driscoll, no one has ever had a more profound impact on my life in worship than you. I remember you saying to me, "In this life you never have too many friends." Phil thank you for your friendship and for showing me the heart of a worshipper. We are not just friends but brothers; I love you bro.

Erhard and Ilse, when God joined

our hearts he gave me the best of friends (iche lebe dich). Charlie, thank you for all your love and help.

Deborah Poulalion and the staff at Creation House, you are a blessing to work with.

John Mason, God so used you to minister to my heart in writing this book. Thank you for your words of wisdom and making a dream come true.

Acknowledgment to Benny

My life has been so blessed as I have sat under the ministry of my brother Benny Hinn. I have learned lessons I could never be taught in a classroom. I am so grateful for those early years of serving him and the church. I remember pleading with him and saying, "Please let me preach; I really think I am ready." But God used him to speak many times to my heart. He would always say, "Sam, if I am the one to promote you, then God is not in it. You have to wait for God to make room for your gift, not me."

This was a great lesson to learn. If man gives it to you, then man can take it away. If a church gives it to you, then that church can take it away. But when God gives it to you, no one can take it away.

Today I have much to be grateful for. God gave me a wonderful example to follow. He has been my brother, my friend and my pastor. As a man he could never change me, but he loved me enough to lead me to the One who could transform my life.

Benny, thank you for allowing me to serve you and the great ministry God has given you. I will never forget giving my heart to Jesus while I was sitting in your room reading your Bible. You came in and took me by the hand and introduced me to the One whom we both now serve. Thank you for all that you have been to me over the years, and I love you with all my heart.

Contents

Foreword

Worship is vital to our existence as Christians because it serves as a doorway into God's presence. Through worship we can enter the very throne room of heaven and bow before God Almighty, the Creator of the universe.

Worship ushers us into a new and greater level of intimacy with the Father. I have discovered that the things on earth grow dim as we spend time in His presence. A once distant God is suddenly closer than our next breath and nothing can draw us away from His glory.

Worship is a vital part of my brother Sam's walk with the Lord. His love for the Lord has been apparent to me since I heard him pray this prayer in his early teens "Lord Jesus, come into my heart, lock Yourself in and throw away the key." That simple invitation was the beginning of a life of loving devotion and service to the Lord.

For the past ten years Sam has served on the pastoral staff of our church here in Orlando, Florida. Whether in the privacy of his home or working in the ministry, I have seen in him a heart which longs to know God more, one which overflows with adoration and worship for the Master.

Changed In His Presence shares some dynamic principles which Sam has learned about worship, as well as many personal experiences about the topic. As you read the pages of this book, take time to let its message sink deep into your being. Allow these thoughts to challenge you and help you discover the ecstasy of time with the Lord. Focus on the Lord, and begin to see yourself in the light of His glory and grace. When you do, you will experience a most amazing, supernatural transformation — you will be *changed in His presence.*

Benny Hinn

O n e

The Call to Worship

On Monday in December 1986 I prepared to lead the early morning
prayer meeting, which was part of my
responsibility as a pastor at Orlando
Christian Center.

Though we had this meeting every
week, I had a very different feeling
about this one. I had no idea what to
expect. I thought maybe I just wasn't
feeling well.

I was part of a great church and a flourishing ministry. God had also blessed me with a beautiful wife and a new baby daughter, yet in the deep recesses of my heart there was a longing and hope that God was about to do something I knew I needed. I was hungry for a move of God.

I got into my office for my usual preparation and began to pray. I was telling the Lord how much I loved him and needed Him. Time seemed to fly by and before I knew it, it was time to go downstairs for the meeting. As I walked through the sanctuary of the church I began to weep and felt the presence of God touching me in a very unusual way. I got to the door of the meeting room, and as I put my hand on the handle the Spirit of God spoke to me more clearly than I have ever heard. He said to me, "I want you to worship Me this morning."

I said, "Lord, I really don't know how to worship you." I walked into the room where about one hundred people were gathered for prayer and told them what the Lord had spoken to my heart.

Even as I talked to the people I prayed silently, "But, Lord, how can I worship in front of these people? I'm a lousy singer!" Singing was the only way I knew to worship at that time. To me worship was just singing all the Christian songs you knew. I was not a worship leader or musician. In fact, I could barely carry a tune. Yet in my hunger and desperation for God I knew I couldn't worry about my ability. I just had to worship Him.

I told the people who had gathered for prayer that morning that we were going to worship God until He came. I was hoping He would come quickly so the people would not have to suffer through my singing too long.

So, we began to sing. We sang all my favorite songs, one after the next, waiting for Him to come and touch us. After about forty-five minutes I had finished all the songs I knew, but I began to feel as though someone had turned on the heat in the room. It was getting warmer and warmer, but this heat went right to the heart.

Then the Lord asked me a question that today still rings inside my heart. He said, "Sam, how much do you love Me?"

I said, with tears flowing like a river, "Lord, I love You with all my heart and with all my life."

There was nothing that could have prepared me for what He asked next. He said, "If your wife and baby were taken from you, would your love for Me change?"

(Please let me make it clear that He said, "If your wife and baby *were taken* from you." He never said, "If *I* were to take them from you." I don't believe that is the way He tests our love.)

I wanted to quickly respond to that question, but a holy reverence came over me, and I realized how critical it was for my answer to be honest. I knew it was my choice and my decision to make. At that moment I felt a void in my heart. Could I really love him unconditionally, even if something tragic were to happen? After a few minutes had passed, I was able to respond overwhelmingly, "Yes, Lord, I will love You unconditionally, for You loved me unconditionally."

I have never felt such a tender moment with God as I did then. It was my own decision. My choice. And no one could change it or take it away from me. I was going to love Him regardless of what situation or circumstance came my way.

I wept till I thought I had no more tears to cry. I began to ask for things I had never asked for in the past. I prayed, "Please, Lord, let me touch You and minister to You." In the deepest part of my heart, I wanted to respond to the way He had touched me. I wanted just for one brief moment to have all the angels in heaven stop worshipping Him so I could be the one to minister to Him.

I told Him if He never healed me I would love Him. If He never delivered me, my love would never change. I would love Him no matter what. I just loved Him for who He was to me at that moment.

During this special time with the Lord, I was totally oblivious to the roomful of people I was there to lead in prayer. I remember a holy hush came over all of us, and the next thing I knew I was on the floor crying so deeply it hurt. Again I kept asking for all of heaven to remain still for a moment so I could touch the Lord.

"Please, Lord," I said, "I want to minister to You. Please don't touch me...just let me touch You this one time." My whole body trembled. I thought maybe I was going to die and be with Him forever.

Right after I said all this, the Lord gave me a vision that revealed what worship was all about. As I lay on the floor, the Lord said: "Look to your left."

I looked and saw a clear picture of a man dressed like an old, traditional Santa Claus sitting in a chair with a very large bag beside him. On the other side of the bag I saw children lined up as far as my eyes could see, one after another, for what seemed like miles. I said, "Lord, I don't understand. This man is like a Santa Claus."

The Lord said, "Look again."

When I looked again I could focus on the children's faces. They were such defeated, dejected faces. No smiles or emotion — just expressionless faces. As they one by one came to the man in the chair, he would lift them up on his knee and give them a gift from the bag. The children, though, did not smile or show any signs of gratefullness or love. They simply took their gift and went on, just as emotionless as they had come.

Then I heard the most astounding, thundering voice say to me, "Tell My people that I am not he. Tell them to love Me for who I am and not what I have."

There is no earthly way to describe the intensity of the pain I felt from those words. My body was shaking and trembling. How could I respond?

Again I heard the Lord speak to me and say, "Sam, I want you to look to the right."

As He spoke those words to me, I was surrounded by a holy and piercing light.

It was like a million suns in its strength, and I felt its warmth and intensity as it touched my body. It flooded me with love that was not human. It went right into my heart, and I knew I was in the presence of God.

I cried out from my spirit, "The unholy cannot stand in the presence of a Holy God, Holy God, Holy God!"

I looked to my right, as the Lord told me to do, and saw this beautiful light in the form of a body, sitting. Again I saw children lined up for miles, but this time there was no bag of gifts, and the children's faces were illuminated with light and smiles. I felt their joy.

As I looked closely at the children, I recognized their faces as being those in the room praying with me. I saw the Lord lift each child, put them on His lap and embrace them with love that I could literally feel. He held each child and tenderly stroked the outline of their faces. It was a loving gesture I had seen my wife use with our own children — brushing her fingertips across the child's forehead, down his cheek, and to his shoulder.

I said, "You are so beautiful, Father! I love you! I never thought You were like this. Forgive me!" All during this, He kept embracing child after child, holding them so tightly.

I desperately wanted to respond to this love I felt. "Please," I prayed again, "let me touch Jesus and minister to Him." As I prayed and wept, I felt like He was going to let me do what I had asked. I began to feel as if I were all alone before the Lord, so I sang and sang. My heart was filled with worship in a way I had never experienced before. In the midst of a song, I felt the overwhelming presence of the God all over my body. It was almost electric and numbing.

Now, I knew He was in the room. I was afraid to open my eyes because I completely expected to see Him. I could sense Him right in front of me.

I cried out, "No, Lord, I can't!" I was sure if I would just open my eyes, I would see Him. The fear of God was real. I was lying face down on the ground. When I finally raised my head and opened my eyes, I found myself gazing at beautiful, strong, holy feet.

I honestly thought to myself, "This was a great way to die." Who was I to see such a man, so full of love for His people? Then I felt hands underneath my shoulders, pulling me to my feet and helping me stand up. His chest was at my eye level. I could not see His face, but-oh-how I knew it was Him! The only words I could use to describe what I saw would be *strength* and *love*.

I knew He was about to give me the desire of my heart — that which I had asked for continually during my worship — that I might touch Him and minister to Him.

I said to Him, "Lord, I am so glad You have a glorified body, because I want to give You the best hug You have ever had, and I don't want to bruise You."

I stretched my arms to embrace Him and heard Him say, "Sam, minister to Me."

As I hugged Him I could feel tears hit my shoulder. Each tear fell with such force that it seemed to weigh a few pounds. I said to Him, "Lord, who has hurt you?"

Again He replied, "Sam, just minister to Me."

After that moment, I felt myself gently deposited back on the floor. I lay on the floor and cried for a couple hours.

What Did It Mean?

I had that vision nine years ago, yet it's as clear to me today as the day it happened. I have never had such a remarkable experience since then.

There may be some who will say, "Who are you to have that experience?" There have been many times when I, too, wondered, "Lord, why did You choose to show that to me?" I have no specific answer, but the Word of God says:

> He who has My commandments and keeps them, it is he who loves Me. And he who loves Me will be loved by My Father, and I will love him and manifest Myself to him (John 14:21).

Jesus said if we love Him, He will manifest Himself to us. *Manifest* means "to exhibit in person, appear or declare plainly." I believe the Lord responded to me because I obeyed Him and hungered after Him.

For a long time after that experience, I wondered about the Lord's tears. I think His pain often comes when we refuse to fellowship with Him. The vision of Him gently embracing each child will never be erased from my memory. It must hurt Him when we miss out on the blessing of His presence.

The scene of the blank-faced children who lined up for the gifts made me reevaluate my own motives. Did I come to the Lord for what He could give me? Or did I come to Him so

I could be changed in His presence?

The children who were in the presence of the Lord reflected His glory on their faces. Did I reflect the glory of the Lord?

God's presence exposed my heart and changed my life as I worshipped Him in that morning prayer meeting. My desire for this book is that it will also make you hungry to come into the presence of our Lord.

Being in the presence of a great man can make you a better man. But coming into the presence of the holy God will change you in ways that men never will.

In the next few pages I will share what the Bible says about worship and its purpose in the life of a believer. This includes:

• the biblical pattern of worship

• how worship changes you

• the mercy in worship

• understanding worship in Spirit and truth

• the difference between relationship and fellowship

- God's view of the need for
  service

- how holiness comes as a
  part of worship.

My heart also goes out to leaders in God's church. I wrote a short chapter for them, just talking about all the things I know from personal experience that are so tempting to substitute for God's presence.

Finally, I have learned so much about worship through the ministry of Phil Driscoll that I asked him to share some of what the Lord has shown him.

The Holy Spirit has been so good to me as I have written this book. I pray He will use these words to touch you, too.

What Is Worship?

The foundation of the whole matter of worship goes back to a covenant relationship which was established in Israel's exodus from Egypt and celebrated in the tabernacle.

During the Exodus, the children of Israel saw God's glory displayed like few have ever seen. They watched Him part the Red Sea and send them through on dry ground. Then they saw the sea crash down upon the Egyptian army pursuing them.

I would rejoice after seeing that — wouldn't you? Moses wrote the following song and the people joined him in singing it:

> I will sing unto the Lord, for He hath triumphed gloriously: the horse and his rider hath he thrown into the sea. The Lord is my strength and song, and he is become my salvation: he is my God, and I will prepare him an habitation; my father's God, and I will exalt Him (Ex. 15:1-2, KJV).

Israel's worship was a response to God for His wonderful act of deliverance. Worship then is our response to God for His faithfulness in delivering us.

Worship celebrates the covenant between the Creator and His creation. God made a covenant with Israel on the night of the Passover. If they applied the blood of the sacrificial lamb, they would be in right relationship with God, and God's wrath would pass over them.

As New Testament believers, we are

in a new covenant with God based on the same principle. If we choose to come under the blood of Jesus, our relationship with God is restored.

God's desire in both the old and new covenants is the same: to redeem people back to Himself, to bring them back to their original purpose — fellowship with Him.

Our Lord created us, saved us, redeemed us and He even designed our approach to Him. Worship is our proclamation of being delivered from our sin, our hurts, our shame. Every time God ministers to us, whether it's to set us free from our sin or to heal us, our response is worship.

Have you ever taken time in the day to think about how faithful He has been to you? When you think about all He has done in your life, how often He has forgiven you, how He has ministered life to your heart when you felt like no one would understand — you can't help but worship Him.

Please, would you stop reading this book for a moment and reflect on all He has done, even in the last few days? This would be a great time to thank Him for His salvation and deliverance in your life. Begin to worship Him with a heart of thankfulness, a heart filled with gratitude for His faithfulness.

The things God has done for us give us endless inspiration for worship.

> Many, O Lord my God,
>   are Your wonderful
>   works
> Which You have done;
> And Your thoughts toward
>   us
> Cannot be recounted to
>   You in order;
> If I would declare and
>   speak of them,
> They are more than can be
>   numbered (Ps. 40:5).

For all that God has done, there's only one possible conclusion: worship is His rightful due. As the prophet Jeremiah put it:

> Inasmuch as there is none
>   like You, O Lord
> (You are great, and Your
>   name is great in might),
> Who would not fear You,
>   O King of the nations?
> For this is Your rightful
>   due.
> For among all the wise men
>   of the nations, And
>   in all their kingdoms,
> There is none like You
>   (Jer. 10:6).

27

Worship in the Tabernacle

Worship, the word we use today, comes from the Old English word *weorthscipe,* meaning "worthship" or "worthiness." Worship reveres, honors and expresses the worth of someone or something. Worship is a celebration of the worthiness of God.

It is easy to see how someone views the worth of another person by the attitude they show to them and by how they treat them. Do we show God how valuable He is to us in our worship? Do we show Him how much He is worth to us?

Worship as a celebration to God for His worthiness can be better understood as we take a look at worship in the tabernacle of David. Worship in the tabernacle was performed by skillful musicians. Each service included singing and playing of instruments. David appointed singers and musicians to minister continually — morning, afternoon and evening — before the ark of the Lord. As they ministered, they composed and recorded their spontaneous music, each new song filled with thanksgiving to the Lord.

Worship in the tabernacle of David is best described in 1 Chronicles 16. David had four thousand gatekeepers and four thousand musicians playing

28

praises to God on their instruments (see 1 Chr. 23:5). This host of musicians and singers started each service by giving thanks to the Lord and calling on His name.

Then they proclaimed His name and His deeds in song for all the people of Israel to remember. They sang psalms and spoke of His wondrous works. They gave Glory to His Name.

As the people progressed in their praises, seeking fresh revelation from God, their hearts rejoiced and their strength was renewed. As they called to memory his marvelous works in the past, they were encouraged that He would continue to act in their behalf.

Such worship was spontaneous and full of joy and celebration. Israel became a worshipping nation. Again and again, "all the people said, 'Amen,' and praised the Lord" (1 Chr. 16:36).

In the Psalms of David we see a wide range of passionate adoration to the Lord. The psalms were Israel's response to God. From agony to expectation, from fear to joy. They are filled with adoration, thanksgiving and prayer. Many of these Psalms were borne out of the celebration of worship that took place in David's tabernacle.

Today I love to be in the midst of a large auditorium filled with people celebrating the worthiness of God in their worship. I love to hear a mighty choir singing forth the praises of God to the accompaniment of musicians glorifying God through their instruments. I love to see a host of people, arms raised and faces glowing, singing in unison of the goodness of God.

Our worship is a celebration. Large or small, young or old, whatever our denomination or geographical location — we can celebrate the worthiness of God, and our covenant relationship with Him, through our worship.

Worship From the Heart

One of the joys of having children is that I can help instill in them a love for God. To me, one of the most beautiful sights in the world is watching my little children worship Him.

Each of my children have learned to express their worship. When my youngest boy, Michael, and I pray together we always express our worship at the end. He looks upward and places his little hand on his lips and blows a great big kiss to Jesus, and says, "I love You, Jesus!"

That is worship expressed. Worship that is not expressed is not worship.

So many of us have little understanding of what worship really is. Worship is not dependent upon our abilities or talents. Worshipping God must come from our hearts.

One of my greatest difficulties in my early years of being a Christian was watching people worship and perform all in one act. I would listen to worship leaders place such emphasis on the singing part of worship I thought, "You really can't worship, Sam, because you have no talent to sing."

I would leave church services thinking, "Why am I not able to feel and sense God's presence like they do? What is wrong with me? Is there something hindering God's presence in my life?" The more I asked these questions, the Lord would open my heart to the understanding that worship has to come from the heart and not talent or ability.

Once I understood worship is simply expressing to God His worthiness, I found myself spending hours worshipping in my car, office, home — anywhere I could find some quiet time. God undoubtedly was touching the deep recesses of my heart with His presence.

So often we think God is really impressed by the words of songs we sing. If we are able to make it sound more eloquent, we think it may draw us closer to Him. The part of us God desires most is not what our mouths pronounce, but what our hearts proclaim.

This is expressed very clearly in Scripture. The Lord explained to the prophet Ezekiel how the words of the people of Israel did not match their hearts.

> So they come to you as people do, they sit before you as My people, and they hear your words, but they do not do them; for with their mouth they show much love, but their hearts pursue their own gain (Ezek. 33:31).

The Lord also expressed the same principle through the prophet Isaiah.

> Inasmuch as these people draw near with their mouths And honor Me with their lips,

But have removed their
hearts far from Me,
And their fear toward Me
is taught by the com-
mandment of men
(Is. 29:13).

Worshipping in Church

For many of us, when we hear of worship we think about the "song service" in our churches. This is an important part of our worship life, but always remember it is only a part. You can worship when there are no other people around you. And, of course, you can certainly worship even if there isn't music!

That is not to say corporate worship is unscriptural. The Psalms say:

Praise the Lord!

I will praise the Lord
with my whole heart,
In the assembly of the upright and in the con-
gregation (Ps. 111:1).

One of the greatest struggles today in corporate worship is that people have become an audience. Sadly, the worship in many churches on Sunday morning is a sing-and-sit event, which divides the church into performers and spectators. There is a great need in churches today to encourage the kind of worship which engages the whole congregation.

It seems some churches have forgotten the purpose behind their music. Churches will seek out talented musicians, looking for better music. God is not seeking better music but better worshippers.

The purpose of music in the church is not to fill the building because of the great music. I have known churches to hire skilled musicians who are not even saved, just for the sake of keeping the crowd coming for the great music. A good choir or band does not necessarily elevate worship.

Please understand there is nothing wrong with great talent and skill. It is wonderful to use the gifts God has given us to bless Him back. We should always strive to give God our very best in our worship. But when too much emphasis is placed on talent, we are only going to stir up people's emotions. God is declaring worship from the spirit.

Worship is the heart desiring and adoring the Father. Music is an expression to help draw out the heart of worship. Music is not the end but only the beginning of worship.

God is seeking worship that is not

limited or legalistic, but spontaneous. This worship comes from the spirit, not the vocal chords.

The Spirit of God does not abide in the ritual or legalistic forms. A legalistic form is something we do because of religious obligation or tradition . A lot of times these forms serve an appropriate function, but they can also be distractions for some people. For example, I think it would be great if the overhead projectors would be turned off once in a while. Let people worship God out of their spirit with no one leading them as the musicians do the same; everyone individually singing, worshipping God out of the heart, allowing their hearts to tell Him how much He is worth to them.

Worship is an intimate love relationship between you and God. I believe worship is passionate and full of a holy desire. We need to be expressive in our worship to God with all our hearts, souls and might.

> Jesus said unto him, Thou shalt love the Lord thy God with all thy heart, and with all thy soul, and with all thy mind. This is the first and great commandment (Matt. 22:37-38, KJV).

You don't have to wait for music to play, or for someone to lead you in song. Worship can be your constant, automatic response to God's forgiveness and His grace.

Pure Worship

When you worship corporately, you are affected by your relationship to the people around you. This isn't good or bad. It's just a fact. I want to share with you what the Lord taught me about this issue.

My brother William and I attended the James Robison Bible Conference in 1987. The presence of God was so real, especially during the worship. I had never sensed anything so pure in a corporate gathering. When James Robison made the altar call one night, I ran to the front. I was hungry for more of God.

As I knelt in front of the altar, I felt the same wonderful presence that had touched me in the early morning prayer meeting at my own church. At that time, I asked the Lord three specific questions, one of which I want to share with you. "Why is the worship in this place so pure?" I asked.

The Lord spoke to me and said, "Son, I want you to look around, all around you." I looked around and saw faces, lots of faces.

He said, "There are seven thousand people here from forty-eight different states. Do you know why the worship is so pure? Because they don't know each other. They haven't had time to get angry or bitter with one another. That's why it is so pure."

When a church is full of strife and dissension, the people will not be free to worship. If your relationships with other people aren't right, you're going to have a hard time entering into worship. Jesus says if you have anything against your brother, leave your sacrifice on the altar and go make it right with him (see Matt. 5:24). I urge you, as a member of a corporate worshipping body, to reconcile with fellow believers.

When we are worshipping in a group where we know the people around us, we also need to consciously overcome our tendency to wonder what other people are thinking about us. If we are worried about whether they think we look foolish, then our worship is also inhibited.

In the next chapter I will share with you the experience that brought about the title of this book.

Changed in His Presence

A few years ago I had to travel by plane to minister in St. Martin. As I boarded the plane in Orlando, I was not expecting the Spirit of God to visit me in any special way on my flight, but He did.

As we took off, I put on my Walkman and began to read the Word. During this flight I had a great hunger in me for God's presence. I had come to a place in my life where ministry was no longer meeting the cry of my heart.

I was listening to a worship tape by Kent Henry when I felt God touch me. I began to worship Him and thank Him for His presence, and I literally felt His presence intensify as I continued. The more the Presence intensified, the more my heart melted. I was close to weeping openly on the plane, but I did not care.

Just when I thought I could no longer keep from weeping, I heard the voice of God's Spirit speak to my heart saying, "Son, you are never changed in the presence of a man; you are only changed in the presence of God."

He began to list for me all the great men and women of God I had met during my years of being involved with my brother's ministry and a large church. They were people whom I would always honor. But the Lord showed me right then even though this was a blessing and I had learned some great lessons from these people, I was never changed as a result of being with them.

I then asked the Lord to please reveal this truth in His Word, knowing He will always confirms what He says by His Word. He took me to a verse in 2 Corinthians, which reads:

> But we all, with unveiled face, beholding as in a mirror the glory of the Lord, are being transformed into the same image from glory to glory, just as by the Spirit of the Lord (2 Cor. 3:18).

You are changed from glory to glory as you behold Him. When you come into His presence, His Holy Spirit will change you. We can be prayed for and anointed by these wonderful people, but there is only One who can bring the change we desire.

If you look to mankind to bring change to your heart, you will be left with an unchanged and dull heart. It will have no passion for God. It may have a passion for man, but not for God.

Worship Brings You Into God's Presence

Change comes when you enter into His presence.

How do we come into His presence? Worship is what allows you to enter in and behold Him. Paul said that we see a reflection of God's glory. As we behold it, we are transformed.

Paul knew this from personal experience. A metamorphosis took place in his life after he encountered the Lord

41

on the road to Damascus. He changed from a persecutor of Christians to one of the leaders of the church. Paul took on the likeness, profile and resemblance of the Lord. From glory to glory he was changed.

Look at 2 Corinthians 3:18 from *The Message*:

> Whenever, though, they turn to face God as Moses did, God removes the veil and there they are — face to face! They suddenly recognize that God is a living, personal presence, not a piece of chiseled stone. And when God is personally present, a living Spirit, that old, constricting legislation is recognized as obsolete. We're free of it! All of us! Nothing between us and God, our faces shining with the brightness of his face. And so we are transfigured much like the Messiah, our lives gradually becoming brighter and more beautiful as God enters our lives and we become like him.

When Jesus the Son of God walked on this earth, He was a reflection of God's glory. When we come into God's presence in worship, we will also shine with His glory. We will take His reflection with us wherever we go. People will know you are different, not because you handed them a tract, but because you became that tract.

If you are longing for God to transform you, He will, when you stand in His presence. You do not have to go to church or give a big offering or hear someone preach to experience it. (Though I believe with all my heart it's important to give, assemble with other believers and hear the Word of God preached.) Change does not happen because we have been faithful members or tithers. It happens because we enter into His presence with worship.

Every believer longs to be like Jesus. My dear brother or sister, today as you read this book, if there's a hunger in your heart for more of God, He waits for you to come to enjoy His fellowship. He will make all the changes needed, I promise.

The Purpose of His Presence

The purpose of God's presence is not just to heal and deliver. For those who have experienced these great gifts, realize there is so much more to His presence. He loves us so much. He not only wants to heal and deliver us, but to make us like Him.

My fellowship with God helps me become the husband I need to be, the father my children need and a better pastor to minister to God's people.

One of the things I enjoy doing after I minister is talking with people who have come to the services. I never fail to meet someone who will try to show their spirituality by the way they talk. They want to out-do everyone else by adding a few more "praise the Lord's" or "hallelujah's." Usually I make my conversation brief with that kind of person.

The essence of worship is to touch the heart of God until I reflect the very glory of Jesus. My spirituality is not measured by how long I pray or how many times I can say "praise the Lord" in a conversation but by the purity of my fellowship with God.

The whole reason I'm writing this book is because I've discovered this fact to be true in my personal life. When I spent time with great men, read great Christian books or went to great Christian meetings, I learned a lot. I felt good. I could even impress other people around me. I thought I was making a lot of progress. But when the Lord touched me with His presence, all those other things paled in comparison. I felt the impact in my *spirit* in a way I never had before.

I want to make you hungry to be in God's presence because I know it will change you. There are two wonderful stories in the New Testament about people whose broken lives were restored by being in Jesus' presence. Let's see what they teach us.

Restoring the Relationship

One of the most extraordinary stories in the Word of God is found in John 4. This is the story of when Jesus ministered to the woman at the well. This story gives us great insight into worship.

> But He [Jesus] needed to go through Samaria. So He came to a city of

Samaria which is called
Sychar, near the plot of
ground that Jacob gave
to his son Joseph. Now
Jacob's well was there.
Jesus therefore, being
wearied from His journey,
sat thus by the well. It
was about the sixth hour
[12:00 P.M.]. A woman of
Samaria came to draw
water. Jesus said to her,
"Give Me a drink." For
His disciples had gone
away into the city to buy
food (John 4:4-8).

It's important to understand the city
of Samaria. It was known as a city of
drunkenness, a place of reproach. Jews
only went there for buying and selling.
I believe the only reason Jesus went to
this city was to meet the woman by
the well.

This woman came to the well to draw
water. The desert is very hot around
noon, and she had a natural need for
some water to drink. So did Jesus, and
He asked her to give Him some water
also. The woman said to Him, "How is it
that You, being a Jew, ask a drink from
me, a Samaritan, for Jews have no
dealings with Samaritans?"

Jesus replied, "If you knew the gift of God, and who it is who says to you, 'Give Me a drink,' You would have asked Him, and He would have given you living water."

The woman told Jesus she wanted this living water, but she was skeptical about His ability to supply it. Her question shows she was stuck in her traditions. She asked, "Are you greater than our father Jacob, who gave us this well, and drank from it himself, as well as his sons and his livestock?"

Jesus answered and said to her, "Whoever drinks of this water will thirst again. But whoever drinks of the water that I shall give him will never thirst. But the water that I shall give will become in him a fountain of water springing up into everlasting life."

Jesus was in effect saying, "Yes. I am different. The water I give you is better than the water you can get from Jacob's well."

During this whole conversation with Jesus, the woman's mind was on her natural need. But Jesus knew she needed more than the natural water. She needed a deep touch within her spirit.

This woman had spent her whole life running, trying to satisfy the deep needs of her heart. She had pursued relationships with many men and she was still unfulfilled. She was trying to scratch an itch in her soul (emotions) that was really deep in her spirit.

When the woman asked Jesus for a drink of this water to satisfy her thirst, Jesus knew the need of her spirit. He said to her, "Go, call your husband and come here."

This must have stunned her. What did her husband have to do with water? Jesus started with a natural situation she was in, and when He had her attention, He pointed out her spiritual need. Jesus put His finger on the most sensitive issue of her heart.

"I don't have a husband," she said.

"Right," He answered her, "You have had five husbands and the one you are now with is not your husband."

Wow, talk about getting right to the point! I think at this moment she must have wanted to run, thinking to herself, "Who is this man that is telling me about my life, when all I wanted was some water?"

There is something important I want to point out here. Like this woman, when we stand in the presence of the Master, He will place His finger on the most troubling issues of our hearts. This is because He loves us

49

enough to confront us with the truth.

The woman had been looking for Mr. Right, but her soul was not satisfied with what she had. When she stood in the presence of a real man, the Son of God, she was confronted with the lack in her life.

She responded, "Sir, I perceive that You are a prophet." She continued, "Our fathers worshipped on this mountain, and you Jews say that in Jerusalem is the place where one ought to worship."

She changed the subject! Jesus must have startled her with His knowledge of her past, so she quickly tried to get Him to talk about a controversial issue so He wouldn't expose any more of her life.

Jesus said to her, "Woman, believe Me, the hour is coming when you will neither on this mountain, nor in Jerusalem, worship the Father."

He told her worship was no longer tied to a place. He challenged her traditional worship with spiritual worship.

Jesus explained, "You worship what you do not know; we know what we worship, for salvation is of the Jews." Jesus was emphasizing a great truth: that it's possible for people to have forms of worship (such as attending church) without having a relationship with Jesus Christ.

His next comment to the woman was one of the most significant statements about worship in all of Scripture. In it, He describes our highest calling as believers.

> But the hour is coming, and now is, when the true worshipers will worship the Father in spirit and truth; for the Father is seeking such to worship Him (John 4:23).

Later in this book I devote an entire chapter to explaining what it means to worship in "spirit and truth." But for now, I want to point out how amazing it was that Jesus taught this woman about worship at all.

Remember, she was living in adultery. He knew it, and she knew it. But Jesus didn't tell her to get marriage counseling or to straighten out her life. Even though her house was in turmoil, Jesus taught her to worship the Father.

One of the most troubling things I see in ministry is marriages falling apart. It seems the devil is launching an all-out attack on families. We need to teach people God's principles about marriage and family. But I also think

we need to teach people how to come
into God's presence and let Him change
them.

> The woman said to Him,
> "I know that Messiah is
> coming" (who is called
> Christ). "When He comes,
> He will tell us all things."
> Jesus said to her, "I
> who speak to you am He"
> (John 4:25-26).

At this point the disciples returned
from the city and were shocked to see
Jesus speaking to a Samaritan. This did
not look good to them. The reputation of
Jesus' ministry would be smudged.

> The woman then left her
> waterpot, went her way
> into the city, and said to
> the men, "Come, see a
> Man who told me all
> things that I ever did.
> Could this be the Christ?"
> Then they went out of the
> city and came to Him
> (John 4:28-30).

The woman left her waterpot. She
let go of her past and left her natural
needs behind. She went right away to

the city and said, "Come see a Man."
She did not give her testimony. She did
not want to share at the next women's
meeting. She told people to go see
Jesus. She brought a great satisfaction
to the Lord.

> In the meantime His dis-
> ciples urged Him, saying,
> "Rabbi, eat."
> But He said to them, "I
> have food to eat of which
> you do not know."
> Therefore the disciples
> said to one another, "Has
> anyone brought Him any-
> thing to eat?"
> Jesus said to them,
> "My food is to do the will
> of Him who sent Me, and
> to finish His work" (John
> 4:31-34).

When the disciples asked, "Lord, are
You not hungry?" Jesus responded,
"You have no idea how satisfied I am."
The heart of the Master was filled
when the woman was changed in His
presence. She affected an entire com-
munity.

> And many of the Samari-
> tans of that city believed in

Him because of the word of the woman who testified, "He told me all that I ever did" (John 4:39).

Love should not be lavished on those who are spotless but on those who are abandoned and undesirable. God is longing to reveal Himself to the person who has a willing spirit and a heart that cries out, "I want to know Him!"

Today, if you are searching, but not finding, like the Samaritan woman, I want you to know the greater the need, the greater the measure of satisfaction. How great is your need today for Him? God will allow you in your desperation to taste the dryness so you become desperate for that which is living. Today God is waiting to commune with you. He is the One who is drawing you to Himself.

Restoring Relationship With God

Many times we come into the presence of God so we can tell Him what we need. We are like the woman who came to Jesus asking Him to heal her daughter, who was demon-possessed (see the story in Matt. 15:21-28).

Many have taken this story and taught that it was the woman's faith that made her daughter well. I believe that is only half the truth. The process started with her relationship with God. Once our relationship is right with God, then we can hold fast to His promises.

Let's take a look into this story. First, it's important to notice this woman was not a Jew but a Gentile. She had no relationship with the Master. She came from Canaan to the coast where Jesus and His disciples were staying. When she found Jesus, she cried out, "Have mercy on me, O Lord, Son of David! My daughter is demon-possessed." Jesus did not even reply. He completely ignored her.

Why would He not answer such a cry from a desperate heart? The disciples also rejected her and urged Jesus to send her away because she was making so much noise.

Jesus explained His treatment of the woman to His disciples by saying, "I was not sent except to the lost sheep of the house of Israel." What does this mean?

Look again at how the woman addressed Jesus. She called Him, "Son of David." However, it would only be proper for a Jew to call Him that name. She was a heathen and had no right to appeal to Him as the Son of David. He ignored her request because she appealed to Him to do something for her on the basis of a relationship which she did not have with Him.

However, instead of leaving, she appealed to Him a different way — through worship.

> Then she came and worshiped Him, saying, "Lord, help me!" (Matt. 15:25).

You would think Jesus would respond to her plea at this point. Did He ever! He exposed her hypocrisy. He addressed her directly and said, "It is not good to take the children's bread and throw it to little dogs."

She called Him Lord and He called her a dog! A little dog! I grew up in the Middle East and was told never use this word. This was a very degrading term. But Jesus confronted her with truth. She was a Gentile, and she did not have the same relationship with Him as did those in the house of Israel.

He wasn't mean or uncompassionate. He used this to bring her into a right relationship with Him.

She responded, "Truth, Lord, I am a dog, but even the little dogs eat the crumbs which fall from their masters' table."

She repented of her previous attitude and acknowledged the truth about herself. Her repentance now brought her into a right relationship with Jesus. He commended her, and her daughter was healed at that moment. She came into a right relationship with the Lord, and the result was her daughter's healing.

Over the past number of years, I have witnessed many things in the ministry. I don't think anything has troubled me more than when I see people desiring the manifestation of God's presence but having no desire to know God. They want what He can do for them, but they don't want Him.

Too many believers have a relationship with God that is dependent on what He does for them. They love Him as long as everything is going fine, but what happens to the relationship when things are not going so well? I encourage you to never come into God's presence just because you need something. Come into His presence because you love Him and need Him.

The Lord will use worship to bring you to Himself, and worship will be an evaluating factor. His evaluations of us in worship are always accurate. There are times when I worship God, and God shows me there is something wrong with our relationship. He uses worship to bring me back to a right relationship.

The reason many do not like to worship is because worship exposes us to who we really are. Out of love, the Lord confronts us. Even though He is merciful, loving, kind and gracious, He loves you too much to leave you the way you are.

The Heart of a Worshipper

God has given me a heart driven by mercy and has placed in me a true love for people. I have never been a person who gets mad or angry. I could go the extra mile for anyone. I even love those who can't stand me. I know, however, this is the Lord's doing and not my own. He knew I would need all the love and mercy I could get because He called me to be a pastor.

People have told me, "Pastor, you are just full of the love of God" or "Pastor, pray that God would give me a love for people like He has given you." This could be very flattering, but I continue to remind myself to be humble because it's God's work in me.

One day this very humble and loving guy was taking his son to hockey practice. We got into the love mobile and drove out. I came to an intersection where I was about to make a right turn. The light was red and I was waiting to merge in with traffic. My son was sitting in the passenger seat and while I was waiting I happened to look in the rear view mirror. Charging up behind me was this blue car that was going way too fast. There was no way for it to stop without smashing into the back end of my car.

The closer he got to my car the more fear and anger rose up in me. He ended up on the median and came very close to sideswiping the passenger side. I was really afraid for my son's life. I thought for sure he would wave in apology or something, but he didn't.

Something snapped inside my heart, and an anger raged within me. I caught up to this guy who was driving eighty-five miles an hour. While we were both speeding down the highway, I expressed to him how I did not appreciate his style of driving. I did all those things macho people do while they are trying to get the attention of another driver. I flashed my high beams, blew my horn and yes, even tailgated.

I took a quick glance at my son and saw a fearful and bewildered face looking right back at me, as if to say, "Dad, have you gone crazy?" I had never experienced this type of anger in my life before. We were now very close to the ice rink and I exited the highway. Then the Holy Spirit spoke and said these profound words to my heart:

> What are you doing? What will you accomplish by this? Do you not see what I am doing inside of you? You thought you knew your heart but I am showing you the things I see in you. Everyone thinks you are so loving, but I want you to see that there are things in you I want to remove.

My heart, so full of anger, melted like ice within a few seconds. I began to weep, asking God to please forgive me. I looked at my son with tears in my eyes and asked him to forgive me also.

My heart was so broken that for the next three days whenever I prayed I could do nothing but repent and cry out for His mercy. I never felt so alone as I did during those three days. I would go into my closet and cry asking Him to please remove this from me and wipe out every root of anger from my heart.It was in my closet that the power of the Holy Spirit filled my heart. He ripped the anger out by its roots. That night I ministered at our church and had such a wonderful service. I knew I was free.

Just when you think you know your heart, God shows you how much you don't know.

Give Him Your Heart Every Day

There is a wonderful song I love to sing that talks about purifying and cleansing our hearts.

Worship begins by giving my heart to the Lord daily. It is important that we give our hearts to Jesus at the altar, but it does not stop there. I cannot imagine what happens to a heart that is given to Him only once. Our hearts need His daily cleansing in order to remain pure. God desires to remove whatever would hinder Him from touching us.

Maybe you gave Him your heart at an altar once, but you have not given Him your heart today. I encourage you to begin this wonderful exchange with God. I do not believe it is enough to give Him our hearts only once.

My prayer is that the first thing you do every morning is give your heart to Him. In the stillness of the early hours of your day, roll out of your bed and onto the floor and give Him your heart. It will make your day — and His. The Word declares:

> For the eyes of the Lord run to and fro throughout the whole earth, to show Himself strong on behalf of those whose heart is loyal to Him (2 Chr. 16:9).

When you and I worship God and stand in His presence, there is a loving confrontation between the heart of God and your heart. God allows you to see the condition of your heart. We can't fool God by acting spiritual on Sunday, because He sees us all week long and knows all about us. Worship brings us to a place where we can see ourselves as He sees us.

For the Lord does not see as man sees; for man looks at the outward appearance, but the Lord looks at the heart (1 Sam. 16:7).

Then hear in heaven Your dwelling place, and forgive, and act, and give to everyone according to all his ways, whose heart You know (for You alone know the hearts of all the sons of men) (1 Kin. 8:39).

I will praise You, O Lord my God, with all my heart, And I will glorify Your name forevermore (Ps. 86:12).

Worship Him With the Whole Heart

How do we know we are worshipping with all of our heart? The Bible tells us how to determine the measure of heart worship in the sixth chapter of Matthew.

For where your treasure is, there your heart will be also (v. 21).

What you treasure is reflected by what occupies your mind, will and emotions. If you want to know where your heart is, examine your mind, will and emotions while you worship. What do you think about? Are you delighting in Him?

Revealing the Intents of the Heart

When I had my reality check on the highway a few months ago, I think what probably broke my heart the most was that I thought I knew what my heart was like, but I was so wrong. The moment the Lord really let me see what it was like, I was shocked. I remember saying to the Lord, "No, not me!" I was confronted with truth. I had to deal with it and give Him my heart.

Since then, I have continually asked God to let me see what my heart is like. The moment you think you know, God has a way of surprising you.

> The heart is deceitful above all things, And desperately wicked; Who can know it? I, the Lord, search the heart, I test the mind, Even to give every man according to his ways, According to the fruit of his doings (Jer. 17:9-10).

The Lord will reveal to us the very
intents of the heart. He knows what
we say and why we say it. He cannot
be fooled.

> As for you, my son
> Solomon, know the God
> of your father, and serve
> Him with a loyal heart
> and with a willing mind;
> For the Lord searches all
> hearts and understands
> all the intent of the
> thoughts (1 Chr. 28:9).

God continually searches our hearts
and knows our motives and intentions.
He knows the very framework of our
thoughts. God, out of His love for us,
will confront us with the condition of
our hearts. What is great is that He
doesn't just leave us hanging with that
revelation. He will reveal it so He can
heal it. Your responsibility is to guard
your heart so it's not polluted again.

> Keep your heart with all
> diligence, For out of it
> spring the issues of life
> (Prov. 4:23).

What a powerful thought: Guard your
heart. People buy expensive security

systems to guard things like cars and jewelry and forget about their most valuable asset — their hearts.

Everything I am and everything I say will spring out of my heart. The fruit that comes out of my mouth is what my heart is really like.

> For out of the abundance
> of the heart his mouth
> speaks (Luke 6:45).

We do not like to admit this, but what we say is what we are like inside. I can't remember how many counseling appointments I've had where one person will tell the other, "Come on, you know my heart. You know I didn't mean what I said." The fact is, what we say will always reveal what is in our hearts. Proverbs also says it clearly:

> As in water face reflects
>   face,
> So a man's heart reveals
>   the man (Prov. 27:19).

If you hear things coming out of your mouth that do not glorify God or edify those around you, then there is something wrong with your heart. Get into the presence of God and ask Him to reveal it to you and cleanse you. Allow His Spirit to change you into His image.

When you give your heart to God, you release His Word to begin an operation in you.

> For the word of God is living and powerful, and sharper than any two-edged sword, piercing even to the division of soul and spirit, and of joints and marrow, and is a discerner of the thoughts and intents of the heart (Heb. 4:12).

I remember once while I was preaching about this verse, I had a samurai sword that was pretty sharp and a chunk of ham. I raised the sword, swung it with all my might, struck the ham and ripped it in half in a split second. The people gasped as the sword sliced through the meat. The ham will never be the same. The people saw a visible change.

Imagine the effectiveness of the Word of God that is alive and more powerful and sharper than a sword. His Word not only divides between the soul and spirit and the joints and marrow. His Word discerns the thoughts and intents of the heart. It goes beyond the natural and goes right into the spirit. The Word knows what you have said and why you have said it.

However, after God operates in your heart with His Word, you won't be left in pieces like the ham I chopped apart. The Holy Spirit will come and begin the work of transforming your heart and will make it like His heart. He will intercede for us and will minister to those areas that cause uncleanness to stain our hearts.

> Likewise the Spirit also helps in our weaknesses. For we do not know what we should pray for as we ought, but the Spirit Himself makes intercession for us with groanings which cannot be uttered. Now He who searches the hearts knows what the mind of the Spirit is, because He makes intercession for the saints according to the will of God (Rom. 8:26-27).

Our times of worship are like a mirror in which we can see a reflection of our hearts. Once we see what God sees, we can allow His Spirit to operate and remove the things in us that do not reflect his character.

Come to the Mercy Seat

Following David's example, our worship should not stop because of some struggle or pain. Our worship of God will actually bring deliverance from that struggle or pain. Worship sets the heart free from even the deepest pit and ugliness of sin.

David is a great example of a worshipper because of the way he dealt with his failures — not his successes.

God found what He was looking for in David. He called him a "man after His own heart" (1 Sam. 13:14). Today God is seeking the same from us.

What is it about the heart of David that gave him such a close place to the heart of God? David understood worship was not just exalting God when everything was going well. In the midst of great tribulation David was able to acknowledge God's greatness (see Ps. 10 and many others). Even in his worst sin he could come to the Lord, repent and be cleansed so he could worship God anew (see Ps. 51).

When a worshipper enters into the presence of God, He is welcomed in with one of the most glorious virtues of God, His mercy! In the tabernacle, the lid of the ark of the covenant was called the "mercy seat." The ark of the covenant was in the holy of holies, where the presence of God dwelled. When we come into God's presence through worship under the new covenant, we also encounter the "mercy seat" (see Ex. 25 and Heb. 9:5).

In the Old Testament the high priest could only go into the holiest of all once a year. But because of the blood of Jesus, we have an open invitation to draw near with a pure heart. As the writer of Hebrews says, "Let us draw near with a true heart in full assurance of faith" (10:22).

We can see God's mercy at work in David's life. Here was a king ordained by God to rule a nation, a great hero and role model to many. Yet David had to confess sin and ask forgiveness for that sin. This made him a worshipper of God.

Worship is not only for those whose character is perfect and morally right. God also welcomes the worshipper who is honest, confesses his or her sin and then praises Him as though it never happened. This is what God requires as repentance:

> With what shall I come
>   before the Lord,
> And bow myself before
>   the High God?
> Shall I come before Him
>   with burnt offerings,
> With calves a year old?
> Will the Lord be pleased
>   with thousands of
>   rams,
> Ten thousand rivers of
>   oil?
> Shall I give my firstborn
>   for my transgression,
> The fruit of my body for
>   the sin of my soul?

> He has shown you, O man,
>   what is good;
>
> And what does the Lord
>   require of you,
> But to do justly,
> To love mercy,
> And to walk humbly with
>   your God? (Mic. 6:6-8).

What does God require of us in worship? There has been too much emphasis placed on the methods of worship rather than the heart in worship. God doesn't require that every time I come into His presence I bow my knee or lift my hands. These physical acts of surrender are pleasing to Him, but His first concern is my heart.

What does the Lord seek in you, and what is it He is searching for in your heart? God desires:

- you do justly (live in His divine law)

- you love mercy (for you have been shown mercy)

- you walk humbly before Him.

The Lord requires us to live lives of worship, not just to have times of worship.

> Who is a God like You,
>   Pardoning iniquity
> And passing over the trans-
>   gression of the remnant
>   of His heritage?
> He does not retain His
>   anger forever,
> Because He delights in
>   mercy.
> He will again have com-
>   passion on us,
> And will subdue our ini-
>   quities.
>
> You will cast all our sins
> Into the depths of the sea
>   (Mic. 7:18-19).

I never hesitate to repent because I know God delights in mercy. Always remember no matter how deep you are in sin, it's never too much or too late for God to forgive. If we will confess our sins, God is faithful and just to forgive us (see 1 John 1:9).

One of the best chapters written on the repentant heart is Psalm 51. First of all, before the psalm ever starts, there is a note that reads, "To the chief Musician. Psalm of David when Nathan the prophet went to him, after he had gone in to Bathsheba." By this we know that in this psalm, David was repenting of his sin with Bathsheba.

74

Have mercy upon me, O
  God,
According to Your loving-
  kindness;
According to the multitude
  of Your tender mercies,
Blot out my transgres-
  sions.
Wash me thoroughly from
  my iniquity,
And cleanse me from my
  sin (Ps. 51:1-2).

First, David boldly asked for the
mercy of God. What is the mercy of
God in the life of a believer? The
Hebrew word *mercy* is *chanan*, meaning "to bend or stoop in kindness to
an inferior." David recognized his
inferior position to God. He placed
himself in a position of total yield to
God's mercy.

David then wrote "Blot out my transgressions." Hebrew for *blot* is *machah*,
"to stroke or rub, to erase." He asked
for God to "stroke, erase, rub out my
transgressions, all my rebellion, sin
and trespasses."

"Wash me thoroughly from my iniquity." The word *wash* in Hebrew is
kabac, which means, "to trample; hence
to wash by the stamping with the feet."
When we ask God to wash us thoroughly

from our iniquity, the process is not very pleasant, because it means He will deal with that iniquity as if He were stamping it out with His feet. Praise God, though, when He deals with it, it is done.

David continued His prayer with "and cleanse me from my sin." *Cleanse* in Hebrew is *naqah*, meaning "to be made clean, to be innocent." Don't you love the look on the face of an innocent child? Once we have sinned and rebelled, we can never gain innocence back on our own. But when the Lord cleanses us, He gives us back our innocence.

Then he prayed, "For I acknowledge my transgressions, and my sin is ever before me."

David was responsible for his behavior and fully accepted the guilt.

> Purge me with hyssop,
>   and I shall be clean;
> Wash me, and I shall be
>   whiter than snow.
> Make me hear joy and
>   gladness,
> That the bones You have
>   broken may rejoice
>   (Ps. 51:7-8).

This verse about repentance has special meaning in my life. When I read it the words snow and bones reminded me of a trip I took.

A few years ago I went skiing with some friends of mine in Vancouver, British Columbia. I was there ministering at my brother Henry's church. I had some time off, and some of my friends wanted to take me skiing. I had never skied before and was looking forward to it.

They were all great skiers, and after a few times down the runs I really picked it up. The day was filled with skiing and fun with the guys. More snow was expected in the forecast, so we went back again the next day. I felt pretty confident by then, so when my friends were doing jumps and skiing down the harder courses, I thought, "I can do that." It wasn't long before I fell and broke my collar bone.

It was never set properly, and I still feel discomfort at times. About a year later I decided to see my doctor and ask if there was anything that could be done to fix it. What he said stunned me. He said the only way to fix it is to re-break it and set it right. All I could imagine was the pain it would involve.

Not too long ago while I was in prayer, God reminded me of this situation. He spoke to my heart about the way I had been repenting. Repentance has to go

77

further than conviction. Repentance is painful; there must be ripping away of the old.

A lot of people feel the convicting power of the Holy Spirit and never repent. Weeping does not necessarily mean I have repented. Repentance requires that my old ways be broken and that I am restored as a new person.

> Hide Your face from my
>   sins,
> And blot out all my ini-
>   quities (Ps. 51:9).

God hides His face from your sins — not from you. A worshipper will boldly approach the throne of God in humility.

> Create in me a clean
>   heart, O God,
> And renew a steadfast
>   spirit within me (Ps.
>   51:10).

David did not say, "God, here is my heart. I want you to fix it and make it right." He said, "God take out this filthy, unclean heart and don't even try to fix it. Create a new one in its place. Let this heart be clean, like you are clean."

There's a parallel verse to David's passage found in Ezekiel 36.

I will give you a new
heart and put a new
spirit within you; I will
take the heart of stone
out of your flesh and give
you a heart of flesh
(Ezek. 36:26).

The sacrifices of God are
    a broken spirit,
A broken and a contrite
    heart —
These, O God, You will
    not despise (Ps. 51:17).

I can best explain this in an illus-
tration. Imagine a beautiful crystal
goblet which represents your heart.
Today and every day there is a battle
for your heart. God calls for your heart
to be His, but you may be tempted to
give your heart to another. The moment
you give your heart to another, it is like
someone taking that beautiful crystal
goblet and smashing it on the floor.
Now all that is left is a million pieces.

For some it may take years to pick
up the pieces of that broken heart.
Once you have picked up all those
broken pieces and you find your way
back to God, all you can cry out is, "Can
you do anything with this broken and
shattered heart?" God takes all those

broken pieces. He doesn't glue them back together, but He gives you a new, brilliant crystal to love and worship Him.

David's heart was not clean, and he cried out for God's mercy. Because God delights in mercy, He restored David and He longs to restore you too.

Worship in Spirit and Truth

Before I began writing this book, the Lord spoke to my heart and said to me, "If you will seek Me I will reveal things to you about worship that you have not known."

Every day I committed time to seeking God, because I want the Holy Spirit to minister to you while you read this book. The most wonderful surprise was how God has ministered to me while I wrote. One particular day, the Holy Spirit confronted me about what it is to worship in spirit and truth.

It started on a Tuesday afternoon. Three of our four children were in school and my wife took the baby with her so I could spend the entire day with the Lord. My heart was filled to overflowing with the goodness of God. I spent the entire day with Him and enjoyed His presence. My life and ministry seemed so fulfilled that day — I could not wait for tomorrow.

The next day was Wednesday and I was asked to minister at church that night. I was excited to get into prayer and knew it would not take long to come into His presence. After all, yesterday had been so wonderful.

I think my problems started there. I had a preconceived idea of what God was going to do that day.

So I went into my closet for my time of worship and prayer. My intentions were pure. I wanted to seek the face of God. I assumed my normal position in prayer and I waited on God. I waited and waited and waited and waited. I knew He could not be stuck in traffic. What happened?

Within minutes the pressure was on. I began to feel stressed out. I didn't understand where He could be. Had I done something during the night that may have displeased Him?

There's a certain song I love to sing because every time I sing it I feel His presence. I began to sing that song — and felt nothing. It was like my heart was millions of miles away from Him.

While I was praying I checked my kneeling position to be sure that it was the same as the day before. It may seem silly but I couldn't understand why I felt so empty. All I could do was keep asking the Lord, "Please show me where I missed it."

A little more time passed and I still could not feel His presence. I understand you are not supposed to go by feelings, but I knew something was wrong. I started to do my spiritual gymnastics, all the little things you learn from watching other people pray.

I actually felt under pressure to come into His presence. Have you ever felt stress in your back between your shoulder blades? That was the kind of pressure I was feeling.

I wanted to tell God what He needed to do. I could not bear the pressure any longer. "Lord," I said, "is this what I am suppose to feel like after twelve years in full-time ministry?"

"This is not what it's supposed to be like, God. I have served you faithfully.

I have studied your Word. I have ministered to your people. Is this the result of all of that? I just want to know You, God. With all my heart I want to know You. Please correct me! Do whatever you must. Just don't leave me like this."

Then the Holy Spirit spoke to me and said, "Relax! You are the one who has brought all this pressure on yourself. Do you want to know Me as you have asked? Then study My Word and you will know Me."

My tears flowed, and my heart melted within.

Then He spoke to me again. "You are trying to worship with your outward man when I desire worship in the spirit. You can't substitute your outward man for your inner man. Everything you have done to this point has been done in the flesh. Did I not speak to you and tell you that worship must come from your spirit?"

I realized like never before that my flesh does not please Him. I was trying to please Him by going through the motions, when all He wanted was for me to relax in Him and allow my spirit to worship Him freely.

In one split second all the pressure disappeared. I began to feel His mercy all around me. My words started to flow smoothly. There were no more struggles.

I have made a new commitment to the Lord, that I will never again substitute my outward man for my inner man. How many times have you and I made some kind of commitment to pray more, "I am going to get up a half hour earlier tomorrow to pray." The next day comes and we need just five more minutes to sleep and end up sleeping through our commitment. Worship is not valued by the clock. Worship is to come from the spirit and not the outward manifestation of the flesh.

Some of the most refreshing times in God's presence will come while I am driving in the car. Sometimes while I walk down the street or maybe while I'm in the mall with my wife and children. Worship is not reserved for just sacred places but for one place — the heart.

If you, like myself, have worshipped in the flesh, I pray the Holy Spirit will show you, no matter where or when or how, God desires worship that comes from the spirit.

God Is Seeking Earlier we looked at the story of Jesus meeting the woman at the well. He revealed to her some of the most significant teaching about worship we have.

85

Following is the key verse from that passage:

> But the hour is coming,
> and now is, when the true
> worshipers will worship
> the Father in spirit and
> truth; for the Father is
> seeking such to worship
> Him (John 4:23).

We need to answer three important questions about this verse:

1. Why is God seeking?

2. What is worship in the spirit?

3. What is worship in truth?

I believe this is the only place where you find the expression that God is "seeking" worshippers. Why would this omnipresent God be seeking worshippers? Several scriptures make it clear that there is no place on earth deprived of His presence.

> "Am I a God near at
> hand," says the Lord,
> "And not a God afar off?
> Can anyone hide himself
> in secret places, So I shall
> not see him?" says the

86

Lord; "Do I not fill heaven
and earth?" says the Lord
(Jer. 23:23-24).

> Where can I go from Your
>   Spirit?
> Or where can I flee from
>   Your presence?
> If I ascend into heaven,
>   You are there;
> If I make my bed in hell,
>   behold, You are there.
> If I take the wings of the
>   morning,
> And dwell in the utter-
>   most parts of sea,
> Even there Your hand
>   shall lead me,
> And Your right hand shall
>   hold me (Ps. 139:7-10).

Solomon made this profound statement while standing at the altar of God.

> But will God indeed
> dwell on the earth?
> Behold, heaven and the
> heaven of heavens cannot
> contain You. How much
> less this temple which I
> have built! (1 Kin. 8:27)

Since God's omnipresence fills the
earth, He would be surrounding all

worshippers. So there must be another manifestation of His presence that "seeks out" worshippers. He does not fill the earth with this expression of Himself, but manifests it to individuals. We can actually "enter" this presence.

> Serve the Lord with glad-
>   ness;
> Come before His presence
>   with singing
> Know that the Lord, He
>   is God;
> It is He who has made us,
>   and not we ourselves;
> We are His people and the
>   sheep of His pasture
>   (Ps. 100:2-3).

There is so much time wasted when people come into the presence of God and then leave. We spend a lot of time going back and forth, in and out of His presence. It's no wonder we struggle to get there.

We can stay in God's presence continuously when we worship Him in spirit and truth. God is a Spirit being and those who worship Him must worship Him in spirit and truth. God makes this possible not through human understanding but through the Holy Spirit.

Worship in Spirit

How we need the fire of the Holy Spirit to breathe on our worship. How our spirits need to be stimulated with the Holy Spirit so our worship is ignited with His fire. God's Word tells us, "No man can say Jesus is Lord, but by the Holy Spirit" (1 Cor. 12:3). If we can't say Jesus is Lord without Him, how can we worship in spirit without the power of the Holy Spirit? There must be an impartation of the Holy Spirit into our spirit, enabling us to worship in spirit, God, who is Spirit.

I was saved as a teenager and grew up in the Lord in the Pentecostal/charismatic church, but for many years I did not have a clear understanding of worship in spirit.

I always thought worship in spirit meant speaking in tongues. In the early years of my Christian life, I would be in church and during worship there were times when the presence of God felt thick all around me. At those times I would weep because His love would be so real to me. But without fail, there would be someone standing behind me speaking in tongues so loudly I could not concentrate.

In those days I had not experienced the gift of tongues. All I knew then was that this person behind me was getting on my nerves. I wanted to turn to him and ask him to be quiet, but I did not want to be rebuked. The atmosphere around me would change because I could no longer express my heart to God. I began to wonder if I could ever worship God in spirit.

I believe with all my heart the gift of tongues is a great attribute to my Christian life, but worship is not contingent on the gift of tongues. Worship is to flow out of my spirit to God. We need to remember the benefits that come from being filled with the Holy Spirit are not just speaking in tongues. The Holy Spirit's desire is to fill every believer, enabling him not only to speak in tongues, but to worship God in spirit and truth.

> And do not be drunk with wine, in which is dissipation; but be filled with the Spirit, speaking to one another in psalms and hymns and spiritual songs, singing and making melody in your heart to the Lord (Eph. 5:18-19).

The call of the Holy Spirit is, "Be filled." This is a continuous infilling, with an overflowing of the Holy Spirit.

Worship in Truth

Sometimes even if we understand what it is to worship Him in spirit, we don't know what it means to worship him in truth. We know from David that if we love the Lord with all of our hearts that we are to walk in truth, but what is this truth He desires in our worship? Does God mean when I worship Him I need to be sure not to lie to him? He not only wants me to worship in truth, He wants me to walk in truth. He desires to be worshipped in truth and for that truth to be deposited into my heart.

> Behold, You desire truth in
> the inward parts,
> And in the hidden part You
> will make me to know
> wisdom (Ps. 51:6).

God desires truth in my inward parts, my heart. God is truth and true worship of Him will cause my heart to walk in it. I will speak in honesty, sincerity and true holiness.

> Teach me Your way, O Lord;
> I will walk in Your truth;
> Unite my heart to fear Your
> name (Ps. 86:11).

> Train me, Yahweh, to walk
> straight; then I'll follow

your true path. Put me
together, one heart and
mind; then, undivided, I'll
worship in joyful fear
(*The Message*).

A worshipper in truth is one whose heart is undivided. Truth will unite my heart in worship so that my emotions, mind and will are all focused on Him. I won't have my will intent on worship while my mind is on the football game. Every part of my being is passionately united in expressing myself to Him.

It's important to have both spirit and truth in the act of worship. If you worship in truth then you will come to know the word of God. But worship in the spirit will allow you to come and know the God of that word. These two practices in worship are meant to work together. One without the other is incomplete and can lead to fanaticism. If worship in the spirit goes unchecked with the Word of God, people tend to get too fanatical. Worshipping in spirit without truth is powerless. Worship in truth without the spirit becomes lifeless, spiritless and lacks fire.

God moves in our lives differently every day. A part of worshipping Him in Spirit is giving Him freedom to touch us the way He wants to, rather than the way we think He should. Our aim should be to let our innermost being, our spirit, commune with Him, without letting our flesh interrupt the fellowship.

Sometimes the best opportunities to worship are the times that seem the most unlikely to us. God is always seeking for us. He longs for us to abide in Him — for our spirits to be filled with His Spirit and for our hearts to exemplify His truth.

Praise From the Heart

In my early years of ministry, I was so hungry to learn more about praise and worship I would listen to as many different messages on the subject as I could. I received so much life and inspiration from them. One wonderful man of God made this distinction between praise and worship: "I praise God for what He has done, but I worship Him for who He is."

In many churches today, there is a separation of praise and worship. The order of service in the church is, first we praise Him, then we worship Him, and then we receive the offering. Praise is fast, and worship is slow.

One day God dealt with my heart about this issue. What He showed me was that praise and worship were never meant to be disconnected from one another. Praise and worship work together. If I don't know who God is, I can't really praise Him for what He has done. When I choose to praise Him, I ask Him to bring me into His presence. As I fellowship with Him there and get to know Him, my heart is drawn more and more irresistibly to Him in love. At that point, I worship Him. Praise introduces me to who He is, and worship is when I give Him my heart.

Just as worship comes from your innermost being, so praise also comes from your innermost being.

I believe the real difference between praise and worship is praise is an act of my will, whereas worship flows out of my spirit. Throughout the Psalms David declared, "I *will* praise You."

> I will praise You, O Lord
>   my God, with all my
>   heart,

And I will glorify Your
name   forevermore
(Ps. 86:12).

David determined in advance that no matter what happened or how he felt, he would praise God. One of the greatest examples of this is found in the story of Jacob, Rachel and Leah (see Gen. 29:5-35). This is the first mention of the word *praise* in Scripture.

Praise in the Midst of Heartache

Jacob's father sent him on a mission to find a godly wife from the household of a man named Laban. When Jacob came to Haran, he asked some men at the well if they knew Laban. "Yes," they replied, "and there's his daughter Rachel now, coming to water sheep."

Jacob didn't waste any time trying to impress Rachel. He ran over to the well, rolled away the stone and watered all of Laban's sheep. His mind probably wasn't on watering the sheep as much as it was on Rachel. Then he kissed her and wept.

He told her he was her father's relative, so she ran and brought back her father to meet him. Laban invited Jacob to stay with him for a month.

After a month, Laban asked Jacob

how he would like to be paid for the
work he did for Laban. Jacob loved
Rachel, so he told Laban, "I will serve
you for seven years for Rachel your
younger daughter." Laban replied. "It
is better that I give her to you than
that I should give her to another man."

We need to remember Rachel was
not Laban's only daughter. She had an
older sister named Leah.

> Now Laban had two
> daughters: the name of
> the elder was Leah, and
> the name of the younger
> was Rachel. Leah's eyes
> were delicate [NIV says
> weak], but Rachel was
> beautiful of form and ap-
> pearance (Gen. 29:16-17).

Rachel had a beautiful countenance
and was beautiful to look at. Rachel in
Hebrew means "to journey." Leah on
the other hand was not so attractive.
Leah had a weak eye which must have
affected her appearance. Leah in
Hebrew means "to make weary, to be
disgusted."

With his heart set on Rachel, Jacob
served seven years, but they only
seemed like a few days because of his
love for her.

Stop and think for a minute. There were no machines to lift and remove things, no cokes, no air conditioned offices. Those were seven years of hard, manual labor. I am sure he couldn't wait for the day he would receive his wife. Imagine seven years of waiting for a bride, seven years of preparation and expectation.

> Then Jacob said to Laban, "Give me my wife, for my days are fulfilled, that I may go in to her" (Gen. 29:21).

Although Laban knew Jacob loved Rachel, he realized his older daughter Leah was still unmarried. Tradition demanded that she marry before Rachel. So he planned a deception. He called for all the men of the city to come and have a feast to honor Jacob, the groom. He made sure Jacob had enough to drink so he wouldn't notice the trick he was about to play on him.

> Now it came to pass in the evening, that he [Laban] took Leah his daughter and brought her to Jacob; and he went in to her (Gen. 29:23).

Here is Jacob who can't wait to marry his beautiful Rachel. He has given years of hard labor for this day. All he wanted from Laban was Rachel. But when he pulled the covers off the next morning, he was in for the shock of his life. As the King James version puts it: "Behold, it was Leah."

What a sight! It was she, the one with the tender eye. In anger he confronted Laban. "What is this you have done to me? Was it not for Rachel that I served you? Why then have you deceived me?" Laban made excuses but the bottom line was this: If Jacob wanted Rachel, he had to serve another seven years.

Jacob served seven more years to get Rachel, and all during that time he was married to Leah. But he really didn't care for Leah. She was like never waking up from a bad dream.

Jacob finally fulfilled his obligation to Laban, and Rachel became his wife.

Let's stop for a moment and look at all this from Leah's perspective. Can you imagine what Leah must have felt like? She knew Jacob didn't want her. It wasn't her decision to marry him in place of her sister. Rachel probably hated her, too. I cannot imagine the pain she must have suffered during those years. But though all those

around her rejected her, the Lord did
not.

> And when the Lord saw
> that Leah was hated, he
> opened her womb: but
> Rachel was barren (Gen.
> 29:31, KJV).

God gave Leah four children, but He
originally gave Rachel none. During
Bible times, children were a great honor
for a woman. The Lord honored Leah.

With every birth, Leah cried out to
God. The first boy was named Reuben,
and she said "The Lord has surely
looked on my affliction. Now my husband will love me."

The second boy was named Simeon
and she said, "Because the Lord has
heard that I am hated, He has therefore given me this son."

She named her third son Levi and
said, "Now this time my husband will
become attached to me, because I have
borne him three sons" (Gen. 29:32-34).

What pain to endure! With every
birth she just wanted to be loved.

> Once again she was
> pregnant and had a son
> and named him Judah
> (meaning "Praise"), for she

said, "Now I will praise
Jehovah!" And then she
stopped having children
(Gen. 29:35, TLB).

Here is the first place in Scripture
you will find the word *praise*. It comes
from someone who did not have a lot to
praise God for. Leah gave birth to
Praise. It came out of her innermost
being. She did not let her circumstances change her heart toward God.

Leah had very little pleasure in her
life. Her marriage was a disaster and
she was hated by her own sister. Yet
God chose her to set the standard of
praise in His Word.

Don't allow the storms of life to steal
the praise in your heart. You can always
praise and worship God in the midst of
the storm.

> Though the fig tree may
>   not blossom,
> Nor fruit be on the vines;
> Though the labor of the
>   olive may fail,
> And the fields yield no
>   food;
> Though the flock be cut
>   off from the fold,
> And there be no herd in
>   the stalls —

> Yet I will rejoice in the Lord,
> I will joy in the God of my salvation.
> The Lord God is my strength;
> He will make my feet like deer's feet,
> And He will make me walk on my high hills (Hab. 3:17-19).

Praise is an act of our will, a decision we make in spite of our circumstances. Leah praised God for what He had done for her rather than complain about what He had not done. Praise always causes us to focus on the blessings of God.

Ten

Fellowship With God

I was born in Israel, but my family left when I was seven years old. After I turned twenty, my family and I had an opportunity to return for a visit.

All the way there my mother tried to remind me of all my relatives. I had so many uncles and aunts and cousins it was hard to remember them all. She told me stories about them and kept going on and on about one particular uncle of mine.

"Oh, he is just like your father!" she said. "Wait till you meet him, Son. You will love him because he is so much like your father."

Well, we finally got to Israel and I could not wait to see that uncle. My father was my best friend and if anyone was like my dad, I wanted to meet him. I was so excited as we drove to my uncle's house.

My mother kept telling me stories about him and said, "Remember son, he is your father's brother. He has the same last name as you do. He is just like your father."

So we arrived at my uncle's house, and as my mom knocked on the door all I could think about was how much we would have to talk about since we hadn't seen each other in thirteen years. My uncle opened the door and I couldn't really remember him, but — wow! — did he look like my dad.

I had two hours or so to spend with him and really get to know him. So I began to talk to him about the things my dad and I talked about. I started with sports; he had no interest in sports. I asked him about car racing; he had no interest in car racing. "Well," I thought, "my dad loves wrestling. I'll ask him about that." My uncle had never seen wrestling.

It soon became clear we had absolutely nothing to talk about, and the next hour and fifty-five minutes were going to go by very slowly. We had a relationship with each other and even resembled each other, but we had no fellowship at all. I had nothing in common with him.

Going Beyond Relationship

My meeting with my uncle is the best way I know to describe the difference between relationship and fellowship. Relationship defines who we are, but fellowship defines who we know. I was related to my uncle, but I did not know him.

I wonder how many in the body of Christ have a relationship with God but have no fellowship with Him. They think they know Him because of what others have told them about Him, but they themselves have no real fellowship with the living God.

Relationship does not replace fellowship. What a privilege we have to come and to know the living God! He desires us as much as we desire Him. He longs for our fellowship as much as we desire His. I pray we never lose our hunger to know Him.

I can't count the number of times

people ask the question, "What happens after I have entered into His presence? What do I do then?" I believe there are many things that will happen when you come into the presence of God. But the most important is that we enter into a fellowship with God. The more time we spend in fellowship, the more God changes us to be like Him.

Worship leads us into fellowship with God. That is what we do when we come into His presence.

From the very beginning, God has always sought fellowship with His creation, mankind. When we read the account of Adam and Eve in Genesis, we see a situation where man was given so much, all for him to enjoy, because God loved him and wanted fellowship with him.

On day one God created the light and darkness; day two, the firmament and waters; day three, earth and vege- tation. On the fourth day, the sun, moon and stars were set into order. On day five, the fish and the fowl were created, and on the sixth day He made the animals and man. God created everything for man that man might enjoy His creation.

And God said, Let us
make man in our image,

after our likeness: and let them have dominion over the fish of the sea, and over the fowl of the air, and over the cattle, and over all the earth, and over every creeping thing that creepeth upon the earth (Gen. 1:26, KJV).

Think with me for a moment. God created man so He and mankind would fellowship together. He made all that we read of in Genesis 1 and 2 for this man. Man was given the whole earth to rule. He was sinless and lived in a perfect environment. From creating the earth to making him a wife, God ministered to the deepest needs of this man, all because He loved His creation and wanted fellowship with Him.

I must understand my purpose of existence. I was not created for anything less than fellowship with the living God and to worship Him.

Genesis 3 introduces a catastrophic event. The man and the woman sin against God, the very One who gave them such abundant life. What was really lost in the fall? Many things changed for mankind, but the greatest loss was the fellowship between God and man that was broken for the first time.

Adam and Eve lost their purpose when they lost their fellowship with God. After the man and the woman sinned against God, they found themselves naked and full of shame.

> And they heard the voice of the Lord God walking in the garden in the cool of the day: and Adam and his wife hid themselves from the presence of the Lord God amongst the trees of the garden. And the Lord God called unto Adam, and said unto him, Where art thou? (Gen. 3:8-9, KJV).

God returned to speak with Adam as though He did not know about their sin. "Adam, where are you?" It wasn't as though God did not know what had taken place, but He was seeking Adam because their fellowship was broken.

Adam had lost his very reason for existence — to enjoy communion with God. Because of this, God sent Jesus to die for us. Yes, He came to save us from our sin, but the ultimate purpose for saving us from sin was to restore our communion with God.

If we confess our sins, He
is faithful and just to
forgive us our sins and to
cleanse us from all unrigh-
teousness (1 John 1:9).

Today your fellowship with God can
be restored, as you simply ask God to
forgive you. It is that simple. Just
confess your sins to Him and He will
touch your heart with His love and
forgive your every sin. Once He has
forgiven you, respond to Him in worship
for everything He has done for you.

Substitutions for Fellowship

How many today
really fellowship with
God? We have fellowship
meetings in our homes
and churches. We fellow-
ship with one another, but we sadly
neglect fellowship with the One who
created us for that very purpose. It
becomes so easy to substitute other
things for our fellowship with Him.

This may get me in a little trouble,
but I'm going to say it: one thing people
often substitute for fellowship with
God is study of His Word. We need to
understand it is possible to know the
Word of God yet have no fellowship
with Him. What is important is not
that I spend time in the Word, but that

I spend time in fellowship with God. Never substitute studying the Word with living fellowship with God.

Sometimes we neglect fellowship with God because we are so focused and uptight about finding out what God wants us to do. We are bombarded with seminars, conferences and teachings on "How to Find Your Purpose," "God's Will for Your Life" and so on.

Yet if we spend too much time trying to find our direction, we will miss our purpose. As Christians, we must remember in the midst of all we do for God, our first and most important calling is to know Him, to love Him and to worship Him. This is our purpose, and anything less is not purpose at all.

The very reason God made us was for fellowship. He gave us the ability to know Him and placed within us the instinct to worship Him.

God gave us His loving salvation that we might be His children and be filled with a desire and a passion to love and worship Him. This is why we were not only created but called by His name.

> [Even] Every one that is
> called by my name: for I
> have created him for my
> glory, I have formed him;

yea, I have made him
This people have I
formed for myself; they
shall show forth my praise
(Is. 43:7, 21, KJV).

Today, if you feel like you have lost your purpose, or if you feel like you have no purpose, I want you to know God is longing for you. He has been seeking you wondering what happened to the fellowship.

Worshipping God brings the greatest fulfillment to mankind. There is nothing on this earth that can replace worship of the true God. People search for it in all different avenues of life, but life and purpose is only found in entering into the presence of God in worship. What is experienced in the heart of the believer in that time cannot be substituted or counterfeited.

You Can't Rush Fellowship

Much of our problem today is that our fellowship with God is so rushed. Many have a difficult time staying in God's presence without the thought of rushing to something else. Many worship God with their lips, while they are making vacation plans, thinking about lunch, and watching their watches wondering when the

111

service will end. That is not fellowship with God.

We need to understand it delights Him when we come to seek Him because we want to, not to fulfill a religious obligation. God has been longing for His people to come back to Him, not just to accept Him, but to seek Him.

My heart breaks when I stand in services and see the blank look on the faces of God's people during the "worship time." They seem lost as to why we are gathered together. They are more interested in seeing who is sitting on the front row rather than getting lost in worship. They look around as the worship leader tries to lead them into the presence of God. Sometimes they want worship to end so they can get into the Word.

One time I heard a preacher say to his congregation, "It is more important that I teach the Word than for the people to enter into worship." As I heard him say this, my heart broke. I thought to myself, "Is there anything more important than worshipping God?" This is the reason we were created. I was not created to go to church, though it is important. I was not created to hear a man preach, though it is important. I was created to love and fellowship with the One who created me. The Bible says:

> Thou art worthy, O Lord,
> to receive glory and honour
> and power: For thou hast
> created all things [that
> includes you and me],
> and for thy pleasure they
> are and were created
> (Rev. 4:11, KJV).

David was driven by his desire and passion to worship God. He articulated his feelings in a beautiful way in Psalm 42.

> As the hart panteth
> after the water brooks, so
> panteth my soul after
> thee, O God. My soul
> thirsteth for God, for the
> living God: when shall I
> come and appear before
> God? (Ps. 42:1-2, KJV).

Who put that desire within David? Who put the desire in you? Was it a man or was it a ministry or maybe the church? The answer is an emphatic no. It was God who put the desire in your heart to worship Him.

Some are still worshipping other

things. Some worship money, cars, shopping, houses or other materialistic things. Some may worship football, basketball or hockey. Some may even worship spiritual things like a particular message, or a man of God, or the gift of prophecy or a specific movement in the body of Christ.

God is not after our worship; He is after us. He is not waiting for you to sing another song; He is waiting for you.

He does not need our worship to satisfy some sort of greed. When you really sit and think about it, what can we really offer Him that He does not already belong to Him? My special ability or song is not going to bring Him glory that He has not already received. All of creation is His. The entire earth and the heavens belong to Him. All creatures were made by Him. All anointing, all power and all honor is His.

Have you ever spent ten minutes thinking about the majesty of God or about His vastness? He is omniscient, omnipotent and omnipresent! All-knowing, all-powerful and everywhere at one time! It's mind-blowing to realize the incredible, eternal God is actually seeking after us, true worshippers!

Please remember that God was worshipped from the very foundations of the world. Nehemiah wrote that the hosts of heaven worshipped Him (Neh. 9:6). God was worshipped before man ever came on the scene.

God doesn't need anything from us, but He *wants* our fellowship. He looks for the deep within the spirit of man to worship Him in spirit and truth.

> Deep calls unto deep at the noise of Your waterfalls;
> All Your waves and billows have gone over me (Ps. 42:7).

Deep Calls to Deep

This verse declares that the Deep calleth unto the deep. God is calling to the deep parts of our spirit to come to know the deep things that are in Him.

God will fill our spirits with His springs of living water. Remember Jesus told the woman at the well:

> Whosoever drinketh of this water shall thirst again: But whosoever drinketh of the water that I shall give him shall never thirst; but the

water that I shall give him shall be in him a well of water springing up into everlasting life (John 4:13-14, KJV).

We as God's people desire to see more of God's presence in our lives, churches, homes and nation. But it's not going to happen just by us singing a few tunes. God calls all of us to a deeper walk and a deeper commitment to Him. He wants us to be willing to spend more time with Him so He can pour His divine treasures into our hearts.

Hunger for God

In all my traveling and ministering here and abroad, I've noticed one common desire in God's people. In service I ask, "How many of you are hungry for more of God than ever before?" The people always respond with an overwhelming yes! Whether it is in Germany or in Indonesia, people are hungry. There is a true desire in the hearts of God's people for more of God and less of playing church.

If I were to ask you right now as you are reading this book, "Are you hungry for more of God's presence in your heart and life?" my prayer is that your answer be yes. If not, then I hope

it will change by the time you finish
reading this book.

In all the years I have traveled and
ministered, there has been one desire
in my heart. I continually pray, "Reveal
yourself to the people who are hungry
for you. Open their hearts to give You
pure and undefiled worship."

When we enter into worship, we are
entering into communion with our
heavenly Father and becoming intimate with Him. This is something that
demands our all; all our hearts, our
souls, and our minds.

In the book of John is another verse
that touches my heart in a special way.

> And this is life eternal,
> that they might know
> thee the only true God,
> and Jesus Christ, whom
> thou hast sent (John
> 17:3, KJV).

Knowing Him is more than a man-
sion in glory, more than wearing a
crown. Knowing Him is eternal life. I
am not going to have to wait to die to
experience heaven. I can begin to
experience heaven right here on earth
as I come to know Him. When Jesus
said, "Father, that they might know
You," He is saying that they might

perceive, recognize, become acquainted with and understand You.

King David gave his son Solomon a charge that should be kept by every man and woman. Let's look at it in two parts.

> As for you, my son Solomon, know the God of your father, and serve Him with a loyal heart and with a willing mind; for the Lord searches all hearts and understands all the intent of the thoughts (1 Chr. 28:9).

David urged his son to know his God. Then he told him to serve. This makes sense, because if we don't know God, how can we serve Him? Then David continued:

> If you seek Him, He will be found by you; but if you forsake Him, He will cast you off forever (1 Chr. 28:9).

Worship is the way I seek God. David promises that if I seek God, He will allow me to come to know Him and learn of His ways.

Worship requires an intimate love

relationship with God where I talk to Him and cling to Him with all my heart. That does not mean I become so spiritual that I am no earthly good. But I know God desires our fellowship to be filled with passion. One of the most heart-touching verses in God's Word to me is found in Philippians 3:10:

> That I might know Him and the power of His resurrection, and the fellowship of His sufferings, being conformed to His death.

Paul's greatest desire was to know Him. That too should be our greatest desire.

We're called to go beyond relationship with God, to have fellowship with Him. There is no substitute for sitting at His feet and allowing the deep parts of our spirit to know the deep things within Him. God desires fellowship with the ones He created for that purpose. Our hunger for more of God will be satisfied as we come to know Him.

Worship First, Then Serve

I remember in my early years of ministry, all I wanted was to serve God. I began as a custodian in our church, and even before that, I traveled with my brother.

One of the most valuable lessons I learned was to serve the man of God. This is a great lesson for all those who desire to be used of God. Everybody has a somebody to serve; my somebody was my brother. He was the instrument God used to help prepare me for the ministry. When we serve under someone else's ministry, God can teach us things we cannot learn any other way.

There has been much teaching on the anointing of God. One of the most important things we need to learn is with the anointing of God comes responsibility.

I have been blessed to serve under a ministry which truly understands the anointing of God. I have learned that God makes servants, not leaders. We need to learn to serve God for as long as it takes.

Some people travel many miles to meetings, trying to catch a double portion of the anointing. There are seminars to teach us "The Secrets to the Anointing," "How to Operate in the Anointing," "How to Bring Down Spiritual Darkness" or "How to Prophesy." Advertisments urge us to come to this service or go to that meeting to learn how to stir up our gifts.

The anointing of God is not something that just happens overnight. You can't learn it at a seminar. The anointing comes with years of faithful service.

In reading 2 Kings, you find something great in the life of Elisha. Elisha was not known for his ministry but for his service. When Jehoshaphat wanted a man of God to come with the word of the Lord on his mouth, one of his servants said, "We know a man that poured water on the hands of Elijah. His name is Elisha" (see 2 Kin. 3:11).

I believe God chose Elisha to *succeed* Elijah because Elisha *served* Elijah. In the same way, Joshua served Moses, and David served Saul.

Those who are serving under their pastor need to pray to catch the spirit and vision of their pastor. I learned firsthand the importance of faithfully serving the pastor, and as a result, God has entrusted me with a ministry.

If you desire to be used by God, you need to know it's not right to try to build on another man's foundation. As God places you in another person's ministry to serve, do not start planning your future. Your future is in the hands of God. If you will serve faithfully that man or woman of God, God will be the one to anoint you and give you a ministry. But He will do it in His time when He knows you are ready.

When those serving in a ministry have not caught the vision and spirit of the pastor, they sometimes think the anointing of God is on them as much as on the pastor. They think their anointing is the same as their pastor's anointing. That kind of person views his service as a stepping stone for personal goals.

God does not make leaders. He makes servants who become leaders. My prayer is for a joining between the pastors and the leadership of the Church. There has been too much bloodshed in the Body of Christ. Men and women are called to one place and then leave and start their own work because they cannot get along with the pastor. Too many churches have split because some have not understood the anointing of God and what it means to serve.

This is not meant to put anyone down, but to help you understand the anointing of God builds and doesn't divide. The anointing of the Spirit gives me a greater love for God's servant so when times get tough, I don't leave; I cleave. Cleaving does not mean for a few months but maybe many years.

One of the greatest privileges I have had has been to serve in my brother's ministry for seventeen years. I would not trade those years for anything in this world. During that time I have learned lessons that have helped mold my life in serving God.

The day of one-man ministry must

come to an end. God is bringing together teams of men and women led by the pastor. But we must be careful that once we are in a place of serving, we continue to serve God and not the ministry. Serving a ministry will put you in a place of discouragement and will eventually quench the movement of the Holy Spirit in you.

Service Pleases God

It pleases the heart of God when there is a need in His house and someone stands up and says, "Pastor, I will be glad to serve."

Those who serve as ushers, nursery workers, Sunday school teachers and greeters — those who give of their time to God's house with a pure heart — do so as a part of their worship. God delights in worship that involves service.

> And now, Israel, what does the Lord your God require of you, but to fear the Lord your God, to walk in all His ways and to love Him, to serve the Lord your God with all your heart and with all your soul (Deut. 10:12).

There is a very close connection between service and worship. The Greek word for service, *latreuo,* refers to an offering or service with no thought of reward. It means to minister to God; to do the service of worship in reverence; a service to God with a deep commitment of the heart.

A wise man of God once told me: You can only minister *for* Him if you have ministered *to* Him.

Some people serve God and substitute their service for worship. Worship is relationship and fellowship with God, not mechanics and formulas. We should not be stirred about serving God until we have learned the joy that comes in worshipping God.

Service Can't Substitute for Fellowship

The order is as follows: First I worship, then I serve.

In many churches the opposite is true. There is much service and little worship. What happens to those who get caught up in the performance of ministry? Their relationship with God becomes dependent on performance rather than worship.

Worship is not a matter of mechanics. It enables a believer to know God and to fall in love with Him. If worshipping God is not the main objective of the believer, then the outcome of service is formulas and mechanics.

Don't Be Distracted From Worship

Please be careful of distractions that will keep you in bondage to things that are not important. We all know the story of Mary and Martha — how Martha was busy cooking and cleaning, while Mary just sat at Jesus' feet and heard His Word.

> But Martha was distracted with much serving, and she approached Him and said, "Lord, do You not care that my sister has left me to serve alone? Therefore tell her to help me."
> And Jesus answered and said to her, "Martha, Martha, you are worried and troubled about many things. But one thing is needed, and Mary has chosen that good part, which will not be taken away from her" (Luke 10:40-42).

No matter how needed you are in your particular area of service, you cannot neglect your own fellowship with the Lord. For example, you may be the one person who is very faithful in the nursery. You are so capable and willing that there is a temptation to work during every church service. But if you do, you won't have the opportunity to worship with other believers. You can easily lose heart and become isolated in your ministry.

> Not forsaking the assembling of ourselves together, as is the manner of some, but exhorting one another, and so much the more as you see the Day approaching (Heb. 10:25).

I remember a few years ago when a great man of God prophesied to me. In the word he made this statement, "You can't minister for Him until you have ministered to Him." He did not know about my deep desire to worship and serve God, but God spoke through him to warn me about a trap set for people who wanted to serve God. The trap is putting service ahead of worship.

This is an important principle. I worship first then I serve. There is a tremendous danger when all I do for God is based on service.

Worship requires that I stand in His presence and minister to Him. Never come to the place in your heart where your desire to serve Him is greater than your desire to worship Him. It is in that place the heart gets dry, empty and void of God's presence. Worship is based on my heart's love and passion for Him, not on my performance.

A Special Note to Pastors

God has given me a great love for His servants. In my traveling I have had the privilege of meeting some of the most wonderful men and women of God. These are men and women with such a heart for God.

I want to take a few pages to address issues that are special concerns to pastors and leaders. (However, if you don't happen to consider yourself a pastor or leader, please don't stop reading. I believe you can also benefit from this information.)

In the last few years God has placed a great burden in my heart for smaller churches. I have gone to these churches and ministered and returned home being more blessed than the people in the services. I would come home with even a greater love for God and these men and women.

Sometimes we place too much importance on the size of the crowd or how large our churches are. I have always held a strong opinion that true church growth is not based on numbers. True church growth is measured by how much the people reflect Jesus — His love, grace, mercy, compassion and trust.

I am often asked the question, "How is it that your brother Benny's church is always full and his crusades are packed with people? How do you get those kinds of numbers?" Benny's meetings may seem large now, but I believe with all my heart when revival comes, every church will be full to capacity. The greatest days for the church are still ahead of us.

Growth is not the problem. The problem comes when we want growth so badly we start trying out different "methods" for growth. God does not anoint programs or methods. He anoints men and women. He does not flow through plans. He flows through men and women. We do not need any more formulas for church growth. We need the anointing of the Holy Spirit in our worship, in our preaching and in the hearts of God's people.

We live in a time when people want everything instantly, no preparation needed. Whether it is food, financial success, or even weight loss, we want it NOW! That kind of mentality has sadly crept into the church. People want their healing, deliverance, financial prosperity and spiritual maturity NOW! People want instant results and yet are not willing to spend time in worship. Some people will actually get up and leave a service that is running late because of a move of the Holy Spirit.

Pastors are put under tremendous pressure to be sure the service ends shortly after the noon hour. After all, the people have to get to the restaurants before the rush.

I am sorry to say, that kind of attitude will not touch the heart of God. If we do not touch His Spirit, then His Spirit does not touch us. But if we touch His Spirit, His Spirit will touch us.

Pastors, I pray you never fall into that trap. Never come to a place where you give the people only what they want, but give them what the Holy Spirit has placed in you.

I know pastors have a great desire to see the unsaved come to know the Lord Jesus. We have spent countless dollars trying to reach out to the oppressed. We have made great advances in the methods of evangelism, but we need to recognize worship is the greatest tool for evangelism. As we saw with the Samaritan woman, one true worshipper can affect a whole city for God.

The most important thing we can do as pastors is to keep our own fellowship with God strong. Only then can we give our people what they need. There is a lot of work involved in pastoring, and it's easy to be so busy serving God we neglect our time with Him.

In the chapter on service, I urged you to worship, then serve. We who are in full-time ministry sometimes act as if we are exceptions to that rule. We are not. If all that we do in the ministry is serve, we begin to depend on formulas and gimmicks rather than the anointing of the Holy Spirit. We start to do things to please the people.

Distractions can easily steal your time with God. Even if the distraction is a godly thing, don't let it keep you from spending the necessary time with the Lord to minister effectively to His people.

Come to Him Alone

Draw me, we will run after thee: the king hath brought me into his chambers: we will be glad and rejoice in thee, we will remember thy love more than wine: the upright love thee (Song 1:4, KJV).

There is a great need for us to come alone into the chamber of the King. He who has called us desires us to come alone with Him. Our real need is not to learn about church growth or how to minister in the anointing, but to spend time with Him. Without an intimate relationship with the Holy Spirit, we have nothing to give. Our teachings will be lifeless and bear no fruit.

If we do not worship first, then we stand and have nothing to minister, because nothing has been conceived in our spirit by the Spirit of God. When that happens, our church's worship time becomes a ritual that is empty and tends to steal the move of the Spirit.

But when God deposits His seed in us, there is always something to minister to the people.

The church is swollen with ministry. We have enough activities to last a lifetime. We need to get back to worship and build the house of God on adoration, not business concepts.

John 12:32 says, "And I, if I am lifted up from the earth, will draw all peoples to Myself." This is the best principle for church growth. If we will exalt and lift up the name of Jesus, He will draw all people.

There's a New Sound Coming

Everybody has somebody they look up to. In music and worship that somebody for me is Phil Driscoll. Throughout my life as a believer I have been touched and blessed by his music. Phil is truly one of the most anointed and skillful musicians in the world. I remember when he would come to our church in Orlando, I always prayed to have the opportunity to host and open the service for him. That's how I first got to know him.

Since then, the impact of Phil's ministry on my life has intensified. I really came to know him well while we were in Detroit together. It was a crucial turning point in his ministry, and he called and asked me to come be with him. During that week God built a friendship between us that has meant so much to me.

For many years, Phil had done only one night concerts in churches. He would rarely do two consecutive nights anywhere. His incredibly busy schedule had taken him to eighteen different cities every month for the last ten years. Detroit was the turning point. He was asked to come and minister at a church for five days. He taught every morning and ministered in song. Every service was full of God's glory. God was honoring Phil's faith and his heart to minister to God's people and lead them into His presence. God's move was so awesome. He healed, delivered and broke chains of bondage over people's lives. God was doing a great new work in Phil's life. I celebrated with him for the way God was changing people's lives, but the greatest change was in me.

God used him to lead me to the highest

level of worship I have ever known. My life was changed forever as I sat and listened to this man minister the Word. The body of Christ needs to know that he is as anointed to teach as he is to play trumpet. God has given Phil a deep revelation of worship from His Word.

Worship was imparted into my life in a new and fresh dimension. The fruit that came from those services is a tape called "In His Presence." On it are many of the spontaneous songs that God gave him in those services. It is the most anointed worship tape I have ever heard. My children go to sleep with it playing all night every night. It is worship that is refreshing and never gets old.

I will ever be indebted to this man of God who has influenced my life and ministry. I pray that as you read this chapter, the hunger to worship Him will be sparked in your heart. Phil, there is a new sound on the earth!

In His Presence by Phil Driscoll

Today, I believe that we, as the body of Christ, are in a new day. There is a new wind blowing. I know in my heart there is a new sound coming to the earth. For several years I have felt that God's music should not only be different but life changing as well. If God is who we say He is — full of power, able to do miracles, filled with light — then the music we play to represent Him should reflect that power. Music was created to be a force to worship God. In the same way, worship should reflect the very character and nature of God.

I am not saying that Christians should not play or sing music that isn't anointed. I am fully aware that there will be times to do songs that are pure, lovely and of good report but are not necessarily anointed or full of God's presence. However, the highest calling of music is still to worship and praise our God. We should feel His presence when we sing or hear this music.

I believe that God's music is coming to earth. I cannot tell you specifically how it will be different, but I can tell you it will include the spontaneous. God is the master of creativity. His music in these last days will demonstrate His wonderful creative power. It will be born by His Spirit spontaneously.

As Sam mentioned, about two years ago I was asked to minister for five days, morning and evening, at a church in Detroit, Michigan. In the last ten years of ministry I had rarely ministered two consecutive nights anywhere. I knew this would be a life-changing trip.

I had an intense desire in my heart to lead God's people into His presence in worship. I had also received a word from the Lord that He was going to change my ministry. I called some of my friends to pray for this meeting. Sam was one friend I called. I asked him to come and be with me. Neither one of us was sure what was going to happen.

I began to teach the people what God had taught me about worship. God's presence intensified with every service. We sang. We cried. We shouted. Most of all the worship was totally spontaneous. I sang only a few of my songs with tracks. This was a new beginning in my ministry. I knew the Lord was calling me to go to places for more than one night. He was also calling me to minister to musicians and singers and affect them with His anointing. I knew in my heart that the vision I had longed for had been born.

Music in Worship

One of the greatest needs in corporate worship today is that we must recover the prototype of music that God gave to Solomon. In the time of David the musicians ministered before God continually. There was a constant sound before God.

When Solomon dedicated the temple, he had a whole staff of musicians whose chief job was to minister before the Lord and to be in His presence continually. They caused His power to be released continually.

> Indeed it came to pass, when the trumpeters and singers were as one, to make one sound to be heard in praising and thanking the Lord, and when they lifted up their voice with the trumpets and cymbals and instruments of music, and praised the Lord, saying: "For He is good, For His mercy endures forever," that the house, the house of the Lord, was filled with a cloud, so that the priests could not continue ministering because of the cloud; for the glory of the Lord filled the house of God (2 Chr. 5:13-14).

It is a foundational truth that music causes the presence of God to come.

Music invokes His presence when it's pointed in His direction. In the Old Testament, music was such an integral part of being in the presence of God, yet today to many believers, it's been reduced to an insignificant and small part of worship. It's background noise — filler. Pastors by the thousands will say, "You play two songs, and then I'll come and give the Word."

The reason we are to be filled with the Word is that it teaches us, admonishes us and shows us God's system and plan for our lives. It builds our faith. Jesus was the Word made flesh, and when He walked on the earth His presence was experienced. When we worship God, His presence is experienced. Is worship less significant than the Word? Certainly not. The Word teaches us: "The entrance of Your words gives light" (Ps. 119:130). His word brings light — revelation. Worship brings His glory — His manifested presence.

A lot of churches live under tradition, and their music is defeated before they ever approach God. Their understanding of worship is limited by thinking God doesn't like this kind or that kind of music. Understand this — there are no godly or ungodly instruments. All instruments were created by God for

His pleasure. God is omniscient, all-knowing. He heard and understood all music even before it was created. He heard every note before it was played. He knew every melody, every harmony and every rhythm *before it was*. What makes music godly or ungodly is the spirit of those playing or singing it and the words it communicates.

The Bible says that the stars sang when God created the world (see Job 38:7). Today we have the technology to pick up the sound waves of the stars and rebroadcast them into sounds we can hear. Music is heard continually in the heavens and controls its atmosphere.

Music does two things. It communicates spiritual power or anointing, and it communicates messages. People listen to music with their hearts, not their minds, because it is a spiritual force. When you hear a sermon, there are thousands of words spoken. Music is not built that way. Music can take a word and develop a sound around it so when it's heard the results can be much more powerful than when it is just spoken.

In Him was life, and the
life was the light of men
(John 1:4).

Worship Releases His Power

Have you ever wondered why heaven is perpetual? The Bible says "In Him was life." How does life get out of God and into the heavenly beings in heaven? It gets there through worship. Worship is the common denominator. The heavens are continually filled with worship. That is how the heavenly beings are filled with God's life.

Many believers in this world today are burned out. They have made Jesus the Lord of their life. They read the Bible. They pray, but they're still burned out. They are not walking in the high places because they have never learned how to approach God in true worship. They aren't aware of all the benefits that are received when you worship Him.

When you worship God you have the opportunity to experience everything that pertains to Him and godliness. Every facet of God's character is accessible as you worship Him. When you approach God the way the Bible says to come to Him, in praise and in worship, you experience all that God represents. Not just a part of His character or a part of His nature, but every aspect of His being is accessible to all who worship Him in spirit and in truth. That is why worship is fought so hard by the rulers of darkness and is demanded so greatly by God.

If there's ever been a time in history that God's goodness needs to be poured out on His people, it's now. We've seen great revelation, but we need to experience the reality of His presence. Many times we have to coerce Christians to even clap their hands or shout. It's not that they don't want to, but they don't understand the significance of it. Praise is to be unconditional. It is not just something to do when we feel good. When we do not praise God, we open ourselves up to living in the atmosphere of this world and receiving everything that darkness has to offer. When we praise and worship God it causes us to walk in the atmosphere of heaven and our spirits to be filled with His light and life.

Praise and worship is something you must discipline yourself to do. It's something we must all practice diligently. According to His Word, power is released when you praise God, but in order for it to benefit you over time, it must be continual. The Bible says, "Let the high praises of God be in their mouth" (Ps. 149:6). That is where it is — *in your mouth.*

There will be many times when you

don't feel like praising God; you don't feel like worshipping Him. However, it is the most powerful force to propel you into His presence. When it becomes a discipline, then you will respond in situations of adversity according to the discipline instead of according to the feeling.

When you learn to fly an airplane, especially the more complex ones, you first go into a simulator to learn and practice. In the simulator you see your surroundings outside the cockpit as well as your instruments, gauges and flight controls. It's just like being in the real airplane. The person running the simulator can make anything and everything break on the plane. You have to learn to respond to each emergency out of discipline rather than with a natural reaction. That comes from knowing your operating manual. You have to do specifically what the manual says and in the time frame it says to do it. The first thing you feel when you experience an emergency is fear, whether it's in an airplane or an adverse situation in your life.

As a believer, a child of God, you know that you are supposed to have power, but if you are fighting in the natural there is no way you can win. Praise has to become an act of discipline in your life to the degree that your reactions to situations are immediate and natural. Your praise invites His presence to come into your life — into your seemingly impossible situation, and that's when you can experience His miraculous delivering power.

When you worship God, the moment you step into His presence, His power, ability and Spirit are released in your life. When that begins to happen, no matter what you're going through, you win.

The Father Seeks Worshippers

Yet a time is coming and has now come when the true worshipers will worship the Father in spirit and truth, for they are the kind of worshipers the Father seeks (John 4:23).

Churches today are full of programs, special demonstrations of talent and production. Many churches classify their entire service as a worship service, but often little worship takes place. Consequently, no one's ever changed.

In worship we must approach God with our heart. You cannot worship

146

Him with your mind. In this verse He is telling us there are a lot of temporal worshippers. They endeavor to worship God with their mind, but they always end up being the spectators in a worship service. They only approach God with their intellect. It's abrasive to God. He will not respond to intellect. Whoever worships God must worship Him in spirit and truth.

You will never experience true worship until you learn to worship in your spirit. Until then, worship will seem like foolishness to you. You know there's a God of the universe who created everything. You know Jesus died to give you life and have accepted Him. You believe that He saved and cleansed you. But you thank Him out of a mental attitude. Mental ascent is not worship — it's meditation. In order for true worship to exist, there must be reciprocation — God's presence must be manifested to you. You cannot get into the deeper things of God with your mind. As believers we must approach God, engage our heart into His and be filled with His life. We will literally plug into God's heart and receive from Him His nature, character, goodness and His mercy.

Behold, the eye of the Lord
is on those who fear
Him,
On those who hope in His
mercy,
To deliver their soul from
death,
And to keep them alive in
famine (Ps. 33:18-19).

Is there famine in your life? If you will worship God, you will not experience famine because He will keep you alive.

All music worships someone. If you listen to any song you hear today, you will find that it worships *someone* or *something*.

When you worship you take your energy and life and you give it in that direction. Whoever or whatever you worship you will become like. When you worship God, you become more like Him. When you worship darkness, you become more like the darkness. When you worship a ball player, you want to become like that ball player. When you worship your career, you become greater in that career. Your intentions and your drive are magnified. That's what worship is. It's an intensifier. It magnifies!

If you want to become more like

God, there's only one way. Worship Him with your heart. If you want to operate more in God's anointing and power, there's only one way to do it — worship with your heart. When you do, you become devoted. You can't stop because the draw to worship is too great. The more you worship God, the more you long to come into His presence. The more you worship Him, the greater your urgency to worship again.

Free in Christ Jesus When you continue to stand in God's presence, all of the forces that Satan has tried to put in your life will fail. Whatever they are, they all operate under the law of sin and death.

> For the law of the Spirit of life in Christ Jesus has made me free from the law of sin and death (Rom. 8:2).

When you begin to worship God, you implement the law of the Spirit of life in Christ Jesus in your life. You begin to break free from all of the gravitational pulls of darkness. It will change your life forever. No one will need to beg you to worship God. It's not right to have to coerce people to worship

Him. He is seeking those who are hungry and *want* to worship Him.

I love to talk to young trumpet players who are just learning. I am not interested in the ones that just play trumpet. I am looking for the ones that are hungry, that want to know, "How do you do that?" They are the ones that I'll spend my time with.

It's the same with God. He is not looking for the nominal Christian who accepts Christ, knows he is free from hell and has established his destiny — but is not hungry for more. He may be free from hell, but he will live hell on earth. That's not what God wants. God's Word says that if you worship and serve Him He will bless your bread and water and take sickness from you (see Ex. 23:25). Let's take Him at His word and enjoy His benefits.

Highest Levels of Faith

Everything that has to do with praise and worship is based primarily on the foundational truth of the law of sowing and reaping. When you give unto God of your energy, it causes God's energy to be released in your life. Religion says, "Don't shout, don't dance, don't make a loud sound." The Bible says to make a joyful noise.

Shouting, dancing and joyful noise all require high energy.

The book of Psalms was written to teach us the value and the means of coming into God's presence. When you come into God's presence the scriptural way, you come before Him with singing, you enter into His courts with praise, you are thankful unto Him and you bless His name (Ps. 100:4). Praise is the highest level of faith in the earth. Praise causes tunnel vision in God's direction. When you implement the principle of praise, you will cause yourself to be translated into God's presence and you will cause God's presence to be translated into you. It automatically dispels darkness. It 'stills the avenger' (Ps. 8:2).

The same exact principle works in worship.

> You shall love the Lord
> your God with all your
> heart, with all your soul,
> and with all your strength
> (Deut. 6:5).

To love God with all your heart is to worship Him with all your heart.

You have to give of yourself unto God. You cannot worship Him by sitting in the back and expecting Him to come to you. He will not come for you. He is not looking to come to those who are passive. He is looking for those who will revere and worship Him intently, who will come into His presence, who will engage their heart, who will dare to go before Him and worship Him. When that happens, you cannot stay the same, and you will be changed.

When we worship God, we are lifted into His presence. We grow closer to Him.

> Draw near to God and
> He will draw near to you
> (James 4:8).

When God's presence falls upon you, everything else in your life becomes unimportant. You are lifted above the circumstances and situations you are in, not by faith, but by God.

I am of the opinion that when you begin to worship God you plug into a new level and dimension of life. Could it be that when we, as worshippers, begin to live and exist in that dimension, we will know what it means to be seated in heavenly places?

I have learned many things about God's laws and systems in the thousands of hours I have flown in airplanes. We hear a lot of talk about head winds and tail winds. Head winds go against the jet stream and tail winds go with it. Did you know that when you fly higher in an airplane, you reach a height where there are no more head winds? You reach an altitude where there is never a storm. As long as you have thrust to propel you, your ship will fly through the air faster because there is less resistance.

Think about that in light of worshipping God. The higher we live our lives, the less storms we will experience. The higher that we live in God, the less resistance we will feel and the faster we will fly.

God is looking for true worshippers right now. Be One! You will fly higher, go faster and face fewer storms. You'll ride the high places and enjoy heaven's highest order. Experience and enjoy the presence of the most high God!

To Your Majesty

Lord, I worship You
I glorify your holy name
With sun and moon
and stars
Your wonders I proclaim
Lord, I worship You
You alone are worthy, Lord
King of all the earth
Lord, I worship You

To your Majesty
I will ever lift my voice
And in You I will rejoice
For all You've done for me

To your Majesty
I lift up holy hands
In your presence I will stand
Through all eternity

by Phil Driscoll

Worship and Holiness

I have had two experiences in my walk with the Lord that I would call life-changing.

The first one was the vision I described in the beginning of this book. The second one occurred on a Sunday morning while I was in charge of the altar ministry at my brother's church.

One particular couple had come to visit our church several times, and I had received a number of complaints about them. This couple had taken it upon themselves to minister to our people without ever making themselves known to the leadership. They felt God had sent them to our church to prophesy over the people and had spoken some very strong words against the pastor and the leadership.

I believe strongly in the principle of "know them that labor among you." My policy was I needed to know the volunteers personally before I allowed them to minister at the altar. On Sunday morning I instructed the altar leaders to stop this couple if they tried to minister to anyone.

After the morning service, this man and his wife came to me and argued with me for two hours. By the time it was over, I was frustrated and tired. I had been at the church since 7:30 A.M. and it was going on 3:30 in the afternoon. As I drove away from the church, I decided I didn't want to return for the evening service. I went home, had a bite to eat and laid down to take a nap. While I was trying to sleep the Holy Spirit spoke to my heart and said, "I want you to go tonight."

So I went, though I didn't feel like it. I sat on the platform that night with the rest of the pastoral staff and a guest speaker. After Benny introduced him, the guest speaker took the microphone and began to minister. After about five minutes, he turned around, gave the mic back to Benny and said he felt like God was wanting to do something different.

So Benny began to lead the church in worship. I lifted my hands and joined in. I could hear my brother praying as he walked back and forth. He was quoting David's prayer in Psalm 51. As he walked by I asked the Lord to please do something fresh in me. With my hands lifted upward I felt a pressure on my back, as if I were touched by a large hand that stretched across both of my shoulders.

The center of the palm pushed my head down to the floor. I gasped for air and wept. As I fell to the floor, I cried out to God, "What are you doing inside of me? Did I ask for this? What is happening?" I started to shake and tremble. I knew something great was happening inside of me, but I didn't know what it was.

I heard Benny call out, "Pick him up! Pick him up! God is doing something in my brother!" He then laid his hands on me and prayed and prophesied over me. I felt a pain in my midsection so great I wrapped my arms around my body and doubled over. The pain was so great I gasped for every breath of air.

I again cried out to God, "Please tell me what are You doing in me!"

The Lord spoke and said, "I have just birthed holiness inside of you."

I realized this was the reason for the pain in my stomach.

When I asked Him why, He said, "Because everything that you have desired for Me to do in you is now done."

I lay crying on the floor for more than two hours.

Then God said to me, "Stand, and you will notice you are changed."

There began a desire in me for holiness like never before. My prayer life changed; my desires changed; my entire walk with God changed. But the most dramatic change was in my worship.

Holiness must come first; only then can we offer up pure worship. Our hearts' desire in worship should be, "Lord, make us holy like you are holy."

A few weeks after this birthing of holiness in my life I was ministering in the Bahamas. One night the Lord spoke to me through a vision. I saw what looked like a priest in the Old Testament times. He was beautifully dressed and looked like he was walking from the outer court into the holy of holies. I saw a rope around his ankle and bells at the bottom of his garment.

In the Old Testament, a priest would go into the holy of holies once a year. Wearing a robe with bells on the hem he would offer sacrifices of atonement on behalf of the people. If there was any sin in him, he would die immediately when he entered the holy presence of God. As long as the bells were ringing, those outside would know he was still alive. But if the bells stopped ringing, they knew he was dead. The rope around his ankle was for the people to pull his body out (see Ex. 28:31-35).

The Lord spoke to me as I was looking at this scene and said, "I am not pulling them out but I am going to draw them in. I am putting a rope around my people to pull them in from death to life."

My eyes were fixed on the rope, and I asked, "Lord, what is the rope?"

He answered, "The rope represents the cords of worship. I will draw My people from the outer court into the holy of holies with worship."

God is bringing change to our worship. It will be more than a song being sung. Worship will lead us into the holiness of God, and there we will be changed. The calling of God on every one of us is a call to holiness.

> But as He who called you
> is holy, you also be holy in
> all your conduct, because
> it is written, "Be holy, for
> I am holy" (1 Pet. 1:15-16).

God desires to birth in you His very nature and character. God is holiness, and He requires those of us who desire Him to be holy like Him. Holiness will bring His glory.

Sometimes we place too much emphasis on the physical manifestations of the Holy Spirit. The same power that causes me to fall down will cause me to be changed when I stand up. The Holy Spirit's touch will always bring a new measure of holiness to our lives.

He Is More Precious Than His Gifts

I have four beautiful children, and God has used them to speak to me many times.

One night He gave me a life changing dream about my oldest daughter, Samia. In the dream it was Christmas morning. I was standing in a hallway and at the end was my little girl's room.

I had so many gifts for her, and I couldn't wait to see her face light up when she saw them. I wanted her to know how much her father loved her.

Her door began to open, and she peeked out. I saw her little face light up. Her smile was so wide. I knew she could see the gifts right behind me under the tree.

I crouched down on my knees waiting for her to run into my arms. Her blonde hair was bouncing up and down as she ran down the hallway. I stretched out my arms to embrace her and she ran as fast as she could right past me. She didn't seem to notice me at all. She ran after all the gifts but ignored me.

My heart was broken. I was the one who gave her all those gifts. I was the one who paid the price for her to have them. I turned around to see her unwrapping all the gifts.

Then the Holy Spirit spoke to me and said, "Son, this is the way it is in the church. They want My gifts, but are ignoring Me."

Today many cry out for the Spirit of God. They want the Spirit to give them more faith, joy, peace, healing or deliverance. We must remember that He is not just the Spirit of God. He is the Holy Spirit of God. When we embrace His holiness, He will touch us with His Spirit.

When our hearts desire Him more than all His gifts, God will give us the

Holy Spirit who will help enable us to be holy. David wrote:

Oh, worship the Lord in
the beauty of holiness!
Tremble before Him, all
the earth (Ps. 96:9).

The call to worship is a call to holiness. God is not just calling us to worship Him in the beauty of holiness, but to live in the beauty of holiness.

A Package Deal

When I met my wife and fell in love with her, I got to know her by her first name. I fell in love with Erika. She fell in love with Sam. She didn't get to know me as Mr. Hinn, but by my first name. Then when we got married, she automatically got my last name and everything that belonged to me.

This is also true of our relationship with the Holy Spirit. When we fall in love with Him by His first name, Holy, we will then receive all the gifts that come with His last name, Spirit.

God calls us to live a life of holiness and if we reject this we also reject the Holy Spirit.

For God did not call us
to uncleanness, but in
holiness. Therefore he

162

> who rejects this does not
> reject man, but God, who
> has also given us His Holy
> Spirit (1 Thess. 4:7-8).

Your calling as a believer is to be a holy temple where God can dwell. God is holy and where he abides must also be holy (see Lev. 19:2 and 1 Cor. 3:16-17). The degree of holiness in your life will be the degree of the presence of God. God's Word tells us we were chosen before the foundation of the world to be holy.

> Just as He chose us in
> Him before the foundation
> of the world, that we
> should be holy and without
> blame before Him in love
> (Eph. 1:4).

Our greatest aspiration must be to live a holy life, not to have a ministry or travel the world preaching the gospel. Our calling is holiness, our ministry is worship.

> But seek first the kingdom
> of God and His righteous-
> ness, and all these things
> shall be added to you
> (Matt. 6:33).

God wants you to seek holiness that comes from Him and not by works. God will only expect of us what He himself has given.

There is such a deep hunger in the church today for more of the holiness of God. People are crying out for change. They want to be more like Him. New songs are being given by the Holy Spirit filled with a holy passion and desire to be more like Jesus.

It is God who puts the yearning and desire in our hearts to be holy, and He is the one who satisfies that desire.

> And a highway will be
>   there, a roadway,
> And it will be called the
>   Highway of Holiness.
> The unclean will not travel
>   on it,
> But it will be for him who
>   walks that way,
> And fools will not wander
>   on it.
> No lion will be there,
> Nor will any vicious beast
>   go up on it;
> These will not be found
>   there.
> But the redeemed will walk
>   there (Is. 35:8-9, NAS).

This is an incredible visual picture of holiness. The road to holiness will keep you away from devouring lions (the devil, see 1 Pet. 5:8). The fool won't walk in the way of holiness; neither will the sinner. But that is where you will find the redeemed.

The greater the hunger for holiness, the greater the degree of satisfaction.

E p i l o g u e

My brother or sister, today God desires to touch your heart with His presence. We have spent too much time going back and forth and coming in and out of the presence of God. He longs for us to stay in His presence that we might live our lives in a state of worship to Him. God desires that you live there, not just visit. That's why it says in 1 Corinthians 3:16:

Do you not know that you
are the temple of God
and that the Spirit of God
dwells in you?

God wants to talk to us face-to-face,
as friends. Abraham was called a
friend of God; Moses became a friend of
God. God is jealous for your friendship.

All the people saw the
pillar of cloud standing at
the tabernacle door, and
all the people rose and
worshiped, each man in
his tent door. So the Lord
spoke to Moses face to
face, as a man speaks to
his friend (Ex. 33:10-11).

Think about the idea that God, the
creator of heaven and earth, wants to
be your friend. Jesus told his disciples
in the book of John, "I no longer call
you servants, but friends." He created
us for fellowship, remember?

Notice when Moses and the people
rose and worshipped, each man was in
his tent door. They were worshipping
in their homes. Worship is not an
event limited to the four walls of the
church. Worship begins in the heart,
then the home.

CHANGED IN HIS PRESENCE

When we gather together at a Sunday worship service, we celebrate together what we have enjoyed with Him during the week. Home is the place where He longs to meet with you.

Bring Forth the Oil

I want to remind you of one last story in the Bible about worship. This is the story of Mary of Bethany.

> And being in Bethany at the house of Simon the leper, as He sat at the table, a woman came having an alabaster flask of very costly oil of spikenard. Then she broke the flask and poured it on His head (Mark 14:3).

This woman took her most valuable possession, an the alabaster box of very costly oil, broke the box and poured it on Jesus' head. Worship is bringing our most valued possession, our heart, breaking it open and pouring the oil of our worship on the Master.

There is no greater desire in my heart than for you to stand where angels can only bow. His presence will change you forever.

168

know that God is calling you to worship Him. He longs for you to worship Him, not because He likes your song, but because He loves you. It doesn't matter if you can sing or not; He is just so pleased that you have come.

If God can change me, I know He can also change you. Please don't hesitate another moment. He is waiting. No matter what your heart is like, He can change it and give you a new one.

There is such precious oil inside of you that was meant only for Him. When you pour it out, He is faithful to fill you again and again. If you will anoint Him with your worship, He will anoint you with His Spirit.

I promise when you stand in His presence you will be changed, never again to be the same. Please don't hesitate another moment. Come and be changed in His presence.

SAM HINN MINISTRIES WOULD LIKE TO RECOMMEND THE FOLLOWING TAPE SERIES:

Guard Your Heart

What was in the heart of David that God said, "This is a man after my own heart?" Today God is seeking those same things from your heart. In this series, learn what will happen when you guard your heart and give it fully to God.

Understanding the Anointing of God

One of the greatest truths we need to understand is the anointing of God. What happens to us when God's anointing fills us? What are some of the fruits we should look for? This series answers these and many other questions about God's anointing.

The Glory of God

There is a hunger in the hearts of believers as they cry out for God. Discover the purpose of His glory and how it will shine in your life as you continually seek Him.

For more information on these and other tape series or to contact Sam Hinn write to:

Sam Hinn Ministries
380 So. S. Rd. 434, Suite 1004-130
Altamonte Springs, FL 32714

IF YOU ENJOY THE MUSIC AND MINISTRY OF
PHIL DRISCOLL, MIGHTY HORN MINISTRY
WOULD LIKE TO RECOMMEND THE
FOLLOWING RECORDINGS:

"In His Presence"

"In His Presence" leads us to truly worship Him and escape the influences of the powers of darkness and our circumstances. When we enter into His presence, we are changed as we are filled with His glory and light.

"SELAH"
Original improvisations of the Holy Scriptures

Without a doubt "Selah" is the highlight of all the music I've ever made for my King and my Lord. These spontaneous songs of His Word lift us into a higher dimension. They unlock new windows in our hearts so the power of His Word and presence shines on us.

If you would like to receive
the Most High Newsletter or information
about Phil Driscoll's ministry or music, please
write or call:

Mighty Horn Ministry
P.O. Box 2218
Cleveland, TN 37320
(615) 476-2235